The Stock Market and Inflation

Edited by

J. Anthony Boeckh

Richard T. Coghlan

THE
STOCK MARKET
AND
INFLATION

DOW JONES-IRWIN
Homewood, Illinois 60430

ISBN 0-87094-272-7

Library of Congress Catalog Card No. 81-82913

Printed in the United States of America

1 2 3 4 5 6 7 8 9 0 K 9 8 7 6 5 4 3 2

To
Don Storey

Preface

There is a saying that of the three ways of losing money—on women, horses, and the stock market—women are the most pleasant, horses are the fastest, and the stock market is the most assured. The poor performance of stock prices in real terms, i.e., after allowing for inflation, over the 1970s has convinced many investors of the truth of that cautionary saying.

This book has to do with stock prices and inflation, particularly in the context of the post-1965 U.S. inflation, by far the most powerful peacetime inflation in U.S. history. The book is not designed to provide an automatic key to riches but rather to cast some light on why stock returns have been so disappointing in the United States since the late 1960s and how inflation in the future may affect returns to shareholders.

Using the stock market to beat inflation should prove to be the investment challenge of the 1980s. The assets that performed best during the 1970s as inflation accelerated sharply and became deeply embedded in the economy—precious metals, real estate, and collectibles—cannot be counted on to repeat their past performance because the environment of the 1980s is likely to be very different from that of the 1970s. Moreover, the assets that are now expensive in terms of everything else are not suitable investments for large institutional investment funds and even for many smaller pools of private funds. These assets tend to be volatile in price and/or illiquid. Essentially, the choice available to most investors is among short-term credit market instruments, bonds, mortgages, and equities. Short-term credit market instruments are only suitable as a temporary abode of purchasing power, not as a permanent use of funds designed to meet either contractual or noncontractual long-term needs. Bonds and ordinary fixed-term mortgages have proven most unsatisfactory during a period of accelerating inflation, as one would expect. On an aftertax basis, bonds have been a disaster for all investors, but in particular for investors in high tax brackets. Moreover, many bonds have become illiquid, volatile in price, and, if of lower quality, very risky. Hence, if we are going to remain in a relatively high-inflation, high-tax environment, most large investment funds, whether they like it or not, will have to use the stock market as their principal investment medium for attaining a satisfactory real, aftertax rate of return.

A number of different views have been advanced to explain why the stock market in general has failed to provide a hedge against inflation, and we thought it would be helpful to investors, and to those studying stock market performance, to collect these views in one place. We have, consequently, obtained contributions from most of the leading combatants, and these are presented in alphabetical order. This has provided the writers with an opportunity to review their own position, to comment on the opposition, and to present new evidence to support their case.

The many different and frequently conflicting views may appear confusing to many readers. In the first chapter we have tried to provide a brief guide through this maze, drawing attention to some of the questions that need to be asked in coming to a conclusion and putting forward our own explanation of the relationship between stock values and inflation. The reader should keep in mind that the question of stock market behavior during a period of inflation is highly complex, and for the serious student there is no substitute for doing one's own thinking and research. Our main purpose in pulling together the various points of view, even though they frequently appear to directly contradict one another, is to stimulate thinking on the subject. Better understanding should lead to better investment decisions.

Despite differences in explanations, the broad consensus is that the market is fairly valued. The main dissenting voices are those of Franco Modigliani and Richard Cohn, who think that the market is substantially undervalued and that stock prices will rise sharply if rationality ever returns to the market.

All of the contributors, with the possible exception of Steven Leuthold, believe that the market now discounts present inflation levels—so that if the present rate of price increases is maintained, the market will provide a higher return, possibly on the order of 18 percent to 20 percent, and act as an important hedge against inflation. However, the general view is that the stock market will not provide a hedge against *accelerating* inflation, and this distinction is crucial to understanding the future prospects for stock prices. There is also unanimous acceptance that a decline in the rate of inflation would be good for the market.

The importance of inflation in understanding what will happen in the future is a consistent feature of all the contributions. For this reason we felt that we should provide some guidelines for the future. In the final chapter we outline our views on the effect of inflation on the stock market and on the prospects for the future and we point out the warning signals to look for along the way. This very much follows the approach adopted in the *Bank Credit Analyst,* which attempts to monitor such developments on a monthly basis in order to provide consistent market forecasts.

In conclusion we would like to record our thanks to Cindy Jones and June Riley for drawing the charts, and Linda LaRoche and Christine Sandahl for help with typing and organization. Without them the book would never have been completed.

J. Anthony Boeckh
Richard T. Coghlan

About the Contributors...

In alphabetical order:

J. ANTHONY BOECKH has been editor of *The Bank Credit Analyst* since 1968 and has written and lectured widely on the state of the American economy and the effects of money and credit developments on financial markets. He has a Ph.D. from the Wharton School, University of Pennsylvania. He spent four years in the research department of the Bank of Canada in the early 1960s and lectured in economics and finance at McGill University, Montreal in the early 1970s.

WARREN E. BUFFETT is an eminently successful investor of long experience who made $25 million in the 1960s running Buffett Partnership Ltd., based in Omaha. This company ceased operations at the end of the 1960s but Warren Buffett, and businesses under his control, still maintains interests in over thirty public corporations.

RICHARD T. COGHLAN is editor of *The International Bank Credit Analyst.* He has written two books (*The Theory of Money and Finance,* The MacMillan Press; and *Money, Credit and the Economy,* Allen and Unwin) and numerous articles in the area of economics, finance, and investment. He has a Ph.D. from Cambridge University, and lectured on economics before taking a temporary appointment at the Bank of England to undertake monetary research. After that he worked as an economist for a firm of stock brokers in the city of London.

RICHARD A. COHN did undergraduate work in economics at Harvard and graduate work in finance at Stanford. He has served as Assistant Professor of Finance at both the Massachusetts Institute of Technology and the University of British Columbia and is currently Associate Professor of Finance at the University of Illinois at Chicago Circle. Professor Cohn has done extensive research in the areas of securities markets and financial intermediation and has published widely in academic journals.

RICHARD WM. KOPCKE is an Assistant Vice President and Economist with the Federal Reserve Bank of Boston. His research has been devoted principally to the financial analysis of nonfinancial corporations and banking institutions in the United States. He received his Ph.D. in economics at Harvard University in 1973.

STEVEN C. LEUTHOLD has been actively involved in various aspects of investment and economic research for over 20 years. He is currently Managing Director for Funds, Inc. and special consultant to Piper, Jaffray and Hopwood. He has written extensively on investment topics and recently completed a book entitled *The Myths of Inflation and Investing*, Crain Books.

BURTON G. MALKIEL is Professor of Economics and Management at Princeton University and Dean of the Yale School of Organization and Management. He received his B.A. and M.B.A. degrees from Harvard and his Ph.D. degree from Princeton. After working for the investment firm of Smith Barney and Company, he served on the Princeton faculty from 1963 through 1981 except for the the 1975-77 period when he served on President Ford's Council of Economic Advisors. He is director of the American Finance Association and serves on the boards of the American Stock Exchange, Prudential Insurance Company, and the Vanguard Group of Investment Companies. He is the author of many articles and books including *A Random Walk Down Wall Street*.

FRANCO MODIGLIANI, Institute Professor and Professor of Finance and Economics at the Alfred P. Sloan School of Management of the Massachusetts Institute of Technology, has published extensively on topics covering monetary theory, corporation finance and capital markets, macroeconomics, and international finance. He is the author of seven books, three volumes of his collected papers, and numerous articles for economic journals. He is currently President, American Finance Association, and Vice President, International Economic Association, and a member of the National Academy of Science and the American Academy of Arts and Sciences, as well as a Senior Advisor for Brookings Panel of Economic Activity.

BASIL J. MOORE is currently Professor of Economics at the Wesleyan University, Middletown, Connecticut. He received his Ph.D. from John Hopkins University in 1958, and his research interests have concentrated on the operation and interpretation of financial markets. He has published widely in academic journals, and has published two books (*An Introduction to the Theory of Finance,* and *An Introduction to Modern Economic Theory,* MacMillan, Free Press).

Contents

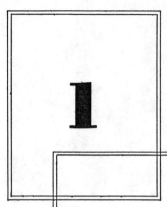

An Overview of the Impact of Inflation on the Stock Market

by

Richard T. Coghlan
and
J. Anthony Boeckh

AN OVERVIEW OF THE IMPACT OF INFLATION ON THE STOCK MARKET

by Richard T. Coghlan
and J. Anthony Boeckh

Over very long periods of time the stock market has provided returns to investors of around 9 to 10 percent. The longer the holding period considered, the larger the contribution of dividends to the total return and the more stable the return. History has shown that stock prices undergo cyclical and secular swings of very substantial magnitude, offering the lure of riches and the penalties of poverty, depending on the timing of purchases and sales. It is not surprising, therefore, that the stock market has been the subject of countless studies designed to unlock the mysteries of stock market behavior and provide predictive tools for capturing above-average returns and avoiding above-average disasters.

Nothing in the history of stock market studies has been more investigated or more controversial than the relationship between inflation and stock prices. Periods of stable prices certainly do not preclude wild stock market cycles, as shown, for example, by the late 1920s and early 1930s. However, one universal characteristic of periods of high inflation is that stock prices fluctuate dramatically in both real and nominal terms. This has been true in all countries and all periods. Generally speaking, stocks have not *always* provided investors with a good hedge against accelerating inflation, although during all inflations, including such extreme experiences as the 1919-23 inflation in Weimar, Germany, there have been periods when stocks outperformed inflation by a wide margin. But on balance, real returns on stocks as a group over a prolonged period of rising inflation have proved disappointing, although certainly not as disappointing as returns on securities with a fixed nominal income, such as bonds and mortgages.

This book does not deal with the question of stock selection but rather with the stock market as a whole in a macroeconomic context. Inflation clearly affects different companies in different ways. Inflation is essentially a disequilibrium phenomenon involving continuing distortions among relative prices. These distortions result partly from time lags. A given impulse of money and credit inflation pushes up different prices and wages at different rates and by varying magnitudes. Moreover, when countries inflate at different rates, relative exchange rates (another price) are distorted, and this in turn feeds back into the domestic price structure, altering relative prices even further. There are also institutional factors which affect relative prices, for example, import controls, unions, and regulation and deregulation of such things as oil and transport. Thus relative prices will shift during a period of fluctuating inflation rates, affecting the growth and stability of earnings. An extreme example during the 1974-80 period was the performance of the oil companies as compared to that of the auto companies.

This introductory chapter has been designed to provide a brief guide to the papers which follow. Each of these papers is concerned in some way with the relationship between stock prices and inflation. Each has a particular point of view which the serious student of the stock market should be aware of. As might be expected, there are points of conflict as well as points of agreement. We have not tried to say who is right and who is wrong. The subject is far too complicated for that. Rather, we have tried to establish a framework within which the different papers can be read and analyzed so as to highlight the points of difference and agreement. We have raised some questions that seemed particularly relevant throughout this discussion and have ended with our own view, which we return to in somewhat more detail in the final chapter. Our main purpose is to stimulate thought and research on the major issues rather than to attempt to supply

4

pat answers where none exist. We do, however, take the view that knowledge is strength and that better understanding will result in improved investment decisions.

Valuation

Stock prices are ultimately determined by shareholders' expectations of a future income stream in the form of dividends. Dividends can only be paid on a sustained basis out of real corporate earnings. There are two other factors that determine how highly shareholders value a given expected income stream. The first is the rate of interest at which any future income stream should be discounted. The second is the expected riskiness of that income stream. In other words, the higher the interest rate, the less a given income stream is worth. Similarly, an income stream which is certain is worth more than one which is uncertain, and along the whole range of possibilities there will be a negative relationship between perceived risk and value.

These relationships can be summarized in the form of a simple valuation equation with the aid of certain basic assumptions. If earnings and dividends are assumed to grow at the same constant rate indefinitely and future dividends are capitalized at the same rate as present dividends, then it can be shown that the expected return on a stock is equal to the current dividend yield, d/p, plus the growth rate of those earnings and dividends.

$$r_e = \frac{d}{p} + g \qquad (1)$$

The same relationship would hold true for the stock market as a whole. In fact, the assumptions are much less unrealistic for the market as a whole because high-growth companies are averaged out with low- and negative-growth companies. The companies which make up the S&P 400 Industrials account for approximately 70 percent of the U.S. nonfinancial corporate sector. Thus those 400 companies are a close replica of

5

the economy, which on balance grows at rates within a relatively narrow band over long periods.

These simplifications allow us to strip away many of the complex details of individual companies and to concentrate on the broad questions of valuation. It should be kept in mind that the main purpose of simplifying the relationships is to derive a framework in which it is relatively easy to see how the main factors affecting valuation work. By definition, any simplification must abstract from much of the detail, some of which will necessarily be relevant for answering certain specific questions.

The nominal or observed rate of interest (r_b), or default-free bond yield, that is relevant for discounting future income streams has two components—the real rate of interest (i) and the expected rate of inflation (π).

$$r_b = i + \pi \tag{2}$$

The required return on equities can also be expressed as the sum of the yield on a default-free bond plus a risk premium (R) which compensates the shareholder for the extra risk of owning stocks over bonds.

$$r_e = r_b + R \tag{3}$$

Combining Equations 1 and 2 into Equation 3 produces the following relationship:

$$\frac{d}{p} + g = i + \pi + R \tag{4}$$

or

$$\frac{d}{p} = i + R - (g - \pi) \tag{5}$$

or

$$p = \frac{d}{i + R - (g - \pi)} \tag{6}$$

This says that the current level of stock prices is positively related to the level of dividends and the expected growth in

6

those dividends and negatively related to the real rate of interest, the expected rate of inflation, and the risk premium required by equity investors.

If we now write α for the proportion of earnings (e) paid out in dividends (d), i.e., the dividend payout ratio (DPR), it is possible to relate the market price to the level of earnings, Equation 7, and also to show the main influences determining the earnings yield (e/p):

$$p = \frac{\alpha e}{i + R - (g - \pi)} \qquad (7)$$

and

$$e/p = \frac{i + R - (g - \pi)}{\alpha} \qquad (8)$$

The reason for setting out a simple valuation model is not to derive a mechanical formula in order to obtain a warranted level of stock prices but rather to have a framework in which to assess how macroeconomic developments affect stock prices. It should be clearly understood that the variables in the model are not independent of one another. When the macroeconomic environment changes, generally speaking, all or most of the variables will be affected. Hence, changing valuation involves simultaneous reassessment of all the various factors. For example, a shift to tight money might raise the real rate of interest, raise the risk premium, lower expected growth rates, lower dividend payments as cash flows of corporations are cut, but at the same time lower the expected inflation rate. Hence, the net impact on stock prices is complex, particularly as the short-term effects of the change in monetary policy may be the opposite of the expected changes in the longer run over which the valuation framework applies.

We want to assess stock market valuation in the particular context of inflation, and this is the primary preoccupation of all the contributions to this book. A reading of the various contributions reveals clearly their basic agreement that inflation is negatively correlated with the stock market. The poor performance of stock prices since 1966 is, without exception, attributed by the authors to the acceleration of inflation from 2 percent in 1965 to the 11 to 12 percent level at the beginning of 1981.

The poor performance resulted from an increase in the earnings yield (e/p—which is the inverse of the p/e ratio) on the S&P 400 and not from a decline in the growth of nominal earnings below the rate of inflation. Figure 1-1 shows clearly the close relationship between the earnings yield and the rate of inflation over the postwar period. The same broad relationship also exists between inflation and the dividend yield, although it is not quite so close, as dividend payouts have tended to slide in recent years. As discussed below, this probably has to do with the growing uncertainty over the stability of the economic and financial environment.

This relationship, however, still has to be explained, and it is at this point that the disagreement begins. The valuation relationships set out above show that the e/p yield should not be affected by inflation so long as the potential trend of future dividends, and therefore earnings, is not disturbed by the rate of inflation and also so long as the real interest rate and the imputed risk premium do not change.

What the evidence suggests is that inflation does cause these various factors to change. Even though real dividends and earnings may appear to be sustained in the initial stages of inflation, there is uncertainty whether they can be sustained in the future. Shareholders' subjective valuation of future returns is, of course, crucial to the pricing of stocks. Clearly, inflation obscures investors' vision of the past as well as the future. It could even cause them to act irrationally or at least to exaggerate the apparent negative impact of inflation on companies and their share prices.

In the papers presented here, various explanations are put forward to explain the poor performance of U.S. stock prices during the inflation of recent years. These explanations focus on the declining dividend payout ratio, declining sustainable

8

Figure 1-1

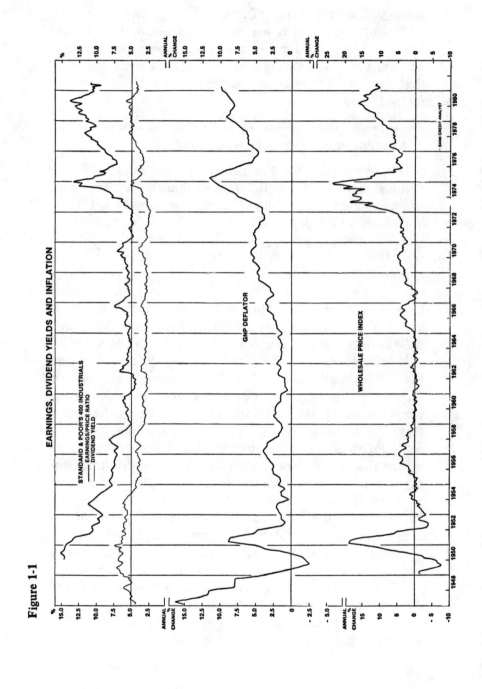

EARNINGS, DIVIDEND YIELDS AND INFLATION

STANDARD & POOR'S 400 INDUSTRIALS
—— EARNINGS/PRICE RATIO
—— DIVIDEND YIELD

GNP DEFLATOR

WHOLESALE PRICE INDEX

* BANK CREDIT ANALYST

earnings, the irrationality of investors, and increased risk and uncertainty. In summarizing these views below, we have emphasized the main arguments that have been put forward, while at the same time drawing attention to certain questions that need to be answered before any final conclusion is reached.

A decline in the dividend payout ratio

One view argues that the dividend payout ratio (DPR) has declined as a result of inflation, and that this has depressed the market price of equities. Its main proponent is Basil J. Moore, who contributed Chapter 7 of this volume. A superficial interpretation of Equation 7, discussed previously, suggests that a reduction in the DPR will reduce stock prices. However, this conclusion depends on other factors not changing. Since the reduced DPR will be associated with a higher percentage of income being reinvested in the company, it should also be associated with the expectation of faster dividend growth in the future, assuming no other changes.

It should be clear that the DPR will be related to the external cost of funds. It is therefore quite feasible for causality to run in the opposite direction: a decline in the market price of stocks as the result of some other cause raises the external cost of funds through the issue of shares, while inflation raises the nominal cost of borrowing and increases risk for the firm, so that the firm could quite rationally retain a larger proportion of its earnings for investment purposes. Thus the mere fact that there is some association between the DPR and stock prices is not evidence of the suggested causality involved in that relationship.

Perhaps the main difficulty with this view is that it does not explain why the dividend yield should rise (see Equation 4). Even if the price of a share falls in line with the reduced dividend being paid, this does not explain why the price should actually fall faster. As some contributors, including Basil Moore, argue, the higher percentage of earnings retained

10

should generally be associated with a higher growth of dividends expected in the future, especially if real corporate profitability has not fallen. It could be argued that this relationship may not be particularly strong, and that expected dividends should not be discounted at the same rate as dividends actually paid out, but these factors only reduce the magnitude of the effect and do not change the direction. And a higher expected growth of dividends in the future, no matter how small or large, should *reduce the dividend yield,* not increase it.

The lower current DPR may well provide part of an answer to the valuation conundrum, but an explanation of the increase in the dividend yield, and the earnings yield, is crucial to understanding the failure of the market to keep up with inflation.

A fall in sustainable earnings

One explanation of the poor performance of stock prices focuses, not surprisingly, on the possibility that sustainable earnings have fallen. As can be seen from Equation 6, even if dividends keep up with inflation, stock prices will increase at a slower rate if the expected growth of dividends falls. Moreover, if dividends are rising relative to sustainable earnings, it is clear that corporate liquidity will become progressively impaired, increasing risk in the future. The crucial issue here is how to measure profits correctly in a period of inflation.

Some adjustments to historical cost-based profit and loss statements are not particularly controversial, such as the need to exclude inventory profits and the need to measure depreciation on a replacement cost basis. Effectively, these adjustments place both inventory and fixed capital on a last-in, first-out (LIFO) basis so that profits will not be artificially inflated when there is no improvement in corporate cash flow. Some analysts make other adjustments. Modigliani and Cohn (Chapter 6), for example, argue that if a gearing adjustment is made to inflation-adjusted earnings to take account of the reduction in real corporate indebtedness resulting from inflation, then earnings have not actually fallen. They hold that once the adjustment is made, real profits can be shown to have continued growing with the economy. Richard Kopcke (Chapter 3), on the other hand, considers it crucial to adjust profit and loss statements to take into account unfunded pension fund liabilities. He also makes other adjustments, including the effect of a rising burden of corporate taxes due to inflation, and concludes that real corporate profitability has fallen as inflation has accelerated.

The actual path of earnings is, of course, crucial to all investors who are trying to form an opinion of the value of share prices. Unfortunately, there is little agreement about the best way to measure true corporate earnings. Steven Leuthold (Chapter 4), like Richard Kopcke, believes that corporate earnings have fallen with inflation. The same view has also been put forward by Warren Buffett in his paper, which first appeared in *Fortune* in 1977 and is reprinted here as Chapter 2. Buffett argues that American corporations are destined to earn a 12 percent return on the historical book value of their assets, so that the return on equity will not increase in line with inflation. He compares this 12 percent equity return with the fixed coupon available on a bond, which is his explanation of why the increase in stock prices has not been able to keep up with inflation. The road back to significantly higher stock values, according to these contributors, is clearly disinflation.

Others have denied that nonfunded pension liabilities or fixed returns on equity significantly reduce real corporate profits. Both Burton Malkiel (Chapter 5) and Modigliani and Cohn reject this explanation, arguing that the quantitative effect of such adjustments remains small, and that, properly adjusted, real earnings have maintained steady growth. They contend that the exception was the rapid growth of the 1960s and not the experience of the 1970s. This view receives some support from the fact that nominal earnings have

12

so far been able to keep up with the increase in nominal income. Since 1975 nominal earnings and dividends have grown faster than the rate of inflation, with average annual increases of 15.2 percent and 12.9 percent, respectively. If real earnings growth was actually deteriorating, then we might expect the nominal increase in dividends and profits to be unsustainable. The rise in the nominal earnings yield and the dividend yield would therefore be only a temporary blip, as stock prices would anticipate a future decline in earnings from this artificially high level. So far, nominal earnings and dividend growth have remained strongly upward.

However, even if real earnings and profits have kept up with the growth of the economy, it still remains necessary to explain why stock prices have been relatively depressed, particularly as reflected in the still very high earnings yield in 1981.

Irrational investors

The argument put forward by Modigliani and Cohn in their contribution to this volume is that investors have been suffering from a form of money or inflation illusion and as a result have consistently undervalued the stock market. Investors have, these authors argue, been making two errors in valuing stocks: first, they have measured profits incorrectly; and second, they have applied a nominal capitalization rate instead of a real rate.

Modigliani and Cohn emphasize the point that, unlike bonds, equities are a claim on real assets. Hence, during a period of inflation the periodic returns to shareholders will be pushed higher by a combination of real growth and inflation. Thus contractual coupon obligations of bonds must be discounted at nominal market rates of interest. Indexed, noncontractual returns to corporate shareholders should be discounted at real rates of interest.

One worrying implication of this view is that it pays to be wrong. Any intelligent investor who did his sums and came

13

up with Modigliani and Cohn's conclusion that real earnings had not fallen, would have picked up all the "cheap" stocks he could only to find his wealth position eroded. On the other hand, the so-called irrational investors who foresaw a simple relationship between inflation and the earnings yield would have done far better.

It also follows that should investors ever learn the truth, stock prices would rise and earnings and dividend yields would fall. Because irrationality is involved, the crucial question of the timing of such learning is impossible to answer. However, the same increase in stock prices would follow from a reduction in the rate of inflation since it is this factor which has, according to Modigliani and Cohn's view, caused the undervaluation.

Most experienced investors have difficulty in accepting the view that they are irrational, at least for extended periods of time. Investors collectively will make mistakes from time to time, placing excessively high or low values on assets. If this were not so, the amplitude of market fluctuations would be much smaller. Information is never perfect, nor is it always very easy to interpret. But this is not to say that investors will not learn, only that they make mistakes, and over time investors will continue to maximize their expected returns for any given risk.

The irrationality hypothesis can never be disproved since no one can measure irrationality. The hypothesis is consistent with all the evidence and can be used to explain anything. Even if true, it is unfortunately of little practical help to investors. The evidence of returns higher than expected over a given interval cannot be used to justify the explanation of irrationality. The market is always providing returns that are higher or lower than expected. For example, from 1932 to 1937 and from 1948 to 1965 the market supplied extra-large returns to shareholders. However, from 1937 to 1948 the returns were pretty dismal, as was true from 1968 to 1974. Irrationality can only be proved if the market systematically supplies returns that vary substantially from what investors

14

seem to require. There is no evidence that this has been the case during the U.S. inflation of 1965-81.

Increase in risk

An alternative explanation put forward by Burton Malkiel emphasizes the increase in risk associated with the recent stagflation environment. Rising inflation combined with lower real growth in the economy has increased the perceived risk of investing in listed corporations. As a result, investors have required an additional premium as compensation for this increased risk. It can be seen from Equation 6 above that an increase in risk is sufficient to keep stock prices down even if nothing else changes for the worse.

On the face of it, this would seem to provide a plausible explanation of what has happened, except for one thing. How is it that the risk premium has risen by exactly the amount required to keep the earnings yield rising with inflation? Malkiel does not provide an explanation of why such a precise relationship should exist. Moreover, he has also suggested that the stock market is efficient in that it reacts to all available information, so that prices follow a random walk and are generally unforecastable. Since Malkiel would not expect to be able to predict prices, his valuation hypothesis seems to take the form of an ex post rationalization for the present level of prices. As an explanation of the past rather than the future, it is also impossible to disprove.

Relating risk to inflation

If an approach based on a variable risk premium is to be of real value to investors, it is necessary to relate risk to something specific so that it can be measured. If inflation were to increase, what would happen to the risk premium, and why? Only if it is possible to answer such questions will such an approach aid investment decisions.

One of the most obvious characteristics of inflation is that it causes uncertainty about past, present, and future earnings. Even with the benefit of hindsight there is no agreement on what exactly has happened to company earnings. Needless to say, forecasting the future is even more difficult. The only certainty is that uncertainty has been increased.

It may well be that real earnings have not declined as a result of inflation, but there are many people who think they have, and that is what matters. Uncertainty about the true state of affairs has increased, and that demands some increase in the risk premium.

Moreover, it could be that inflation creates the expectation that company profitability will be adversely affected *in the future*. Therefore, even if earnings and profits hold up in the present, investors might believe that companies will be unable to maintain this performance. Why should this be the case?

It should be clear to investors that tightening credit adversely affects the stock market. Consider Figures 1-2 and 1-3. The first shows that as interest rates rise, and in particular as the yield gap between long and short rates closes up, the earnings yield also rises. Figure 1-3 reveals that the cause is falling stock prices, as the market moves to anticipate a downturn in the economy which will be triggered by an expected credit crunch, rather than a decline in current earnings. The historic relationship between credit tightening, depressed stock market conditions, and subsequent low levels of economic activity has resulted in the use of stock market prices as a major component of the leading indicator series for the direction of the economy. In the past, less interest rate pressure was required to turn the market. This was not because credit tightening was less important, but rather because interest rates were not the main weapon of monetary control. That role was played by controls on credit, applied either directly or indirectly, primarily through disintermediation caused by Regulation Q ceilings. Institutional developments in recent years have caused greater and greater control

16

Figure 1-2

EARNINGS/PRICE RATIO AND INTEREST RATES

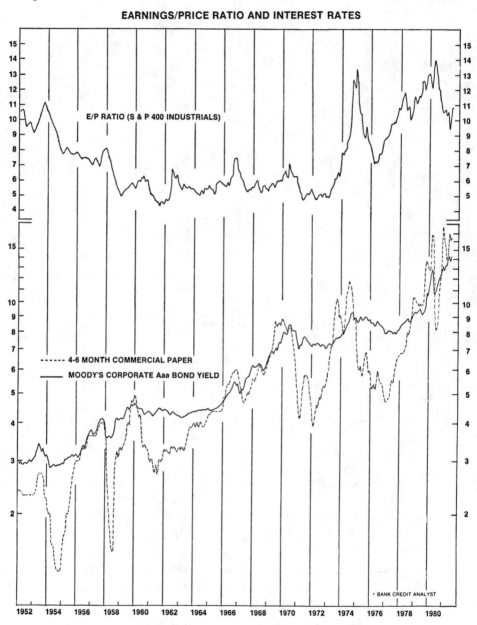

E/P RATIO (S & P 400 INDUSTRIALS)

------ 4-6 MONTH COMMERCIAL PAPER

—— MOODY'S CORPORATE Aaa BOND YIELD

* BANK CREDIT ANALYST

Figure 1-3

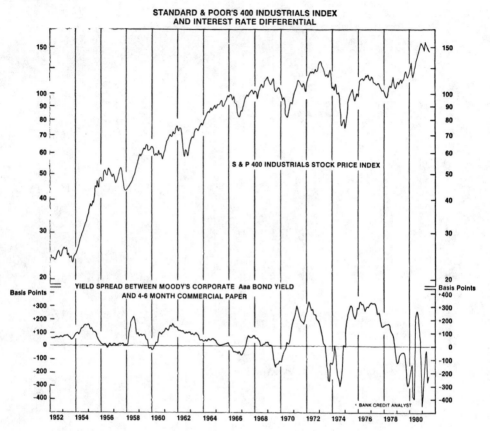

STANDARD & POOR'S 400 INDUSTRIALS INDEX
AND INTEREST RATE DIFFERENTIAL

to come via interest rates, and this process will be carried to its ultimate conclusion during the 1980s through the implementation of the Depository Institutions Deregulation and Monetary Control Act of 1980. Such institutional developments must be taken into account in interpreting and using historical relationships for forecasting stock market trends in the future. This subject is considered further in Chapter 8.

If an investor believes that an increase in the rate of inflation will result in a period of tightening credit, which will depress the economy and company profitability in the future, it is only logical that he should want to discount this in the price he is prepared to pay in the present. Therefore, even though current earnings hold up, prices will fall in *anticipation* of the fall in future earnings, automatically increasing the earnings yield. Although nominal earnings rise with inflation, the credit tightening can be reasonably interpreted as resulting in real declines in earnings before inflation is reduced.

It is dangerous to assume that the problems of inflation are somehow separate from the real side of the economy. In discussions of the effects of inflation on the stock market, the economic consequences of reducing or increasing inflation are generally ignored. Inflation results from pressures created within the economic system and cannot be considered in isolation. It is one thing to talk about the ultimate effects of a lower rate of inflation on the stock market and quite another to discuss the near-term effects of policies which will reduce inflation to that lower level.

Reducing inflation through the application of tight money policies will depress economic activity and company profits, and will result in a sharp increase in the number and value of bankruptcies. As a rule of thumb, investors might consider discounting the earnings resulting from higher inflation, on the grounds that these are only temporary and will be lost in the subsequent correction. This seems an increasingly sensible strategy when the increase in uncertainty about exactly what earnings and profitability are doing under the camouflage of inflation is also taken into account. Because of such anticipatory behavior, tightening monetary policy at the end of the 1970s and early 80s has had much less impact on stock prices than it would have had otherwise (see Figure 1-3).

We have, therefore, arrived at an alternative explanation for why the earnings yield should rise with the rate of inflation. It is not because real earnings in the present have necessarily declined, nor is it because of an increase in risk in the present. The increase in risk is in the future, because earnings

19

are expected to be hit by efforts to reduce inflation. We shall discuss this approach in more detail in the final chapter of the book, and also some additional factors that we think should be taken into account in realistically assessing stock prices during an inflationary period.

Although this approach assumes rationality on the part of investors, the conclusions are virtually the same as those proposed by Modigliani and Cohn under the assumption of irrationality. Lower inflation will produce a lower earnings yield, after the painful correction period. Moreover, if a stable rate of inflation became embedded in the system and no efforts were made to reduce it, then again the earnings yield should decline. This is because the risk of correction, at least for the time being, would be reduced and investors would gradually stop discounting the possibility.

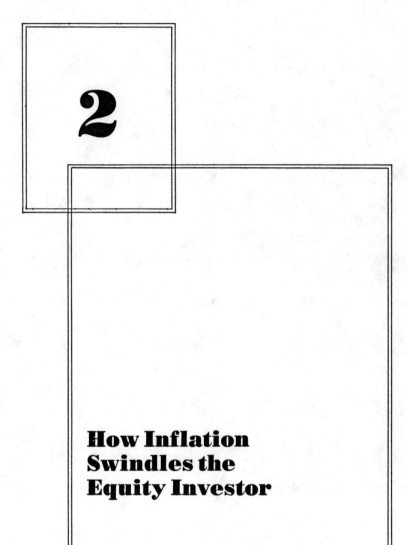

2

How Inflation Swindles the Equity Investor

by

Warren E. Buffett

HOW INFLATION SWINDLES THE EQUITY INVESTOR

by Warren E. Buffett

It is no longer a secret that stocks, like bonds, do poorly in an inflationary environment. We have been in such an environment for most of the past decade, and it has indeed been a time of troubles for stocks. But the reasons for the stock market's problems in this period are still imperfectly understood.

There is no mystery at all about the problems of bondholders in an era of inflation. When the value of the dollar deteriorates month after month, a security with income and principal payments denominated in those dollars isn't going to be a big winner. You hardly need a Ph.D. in economics to figure that one out.

It was long assumed that stocks were something else. For many years, the conventional wisdom insisted that stocks were a hedge against inflation. The proposition was rooted in the fact that stocks are not claims against dollars, as bonds are, but represent ownership of companies with productive facilities. These, investors believed, would retain their value in real terms, let the politicians print money as they might.

And why didn't it turn out that way? The main reason, I believe, is that stocks, in economic substance, are really very similar to bonds.

I know that this belief will seem eccentric to many investors. They will immediately observe that the return on a bond (the coupon) is fixed, while the return on an equity investment (the company's earnings) can vary substantially from one year to another. True enough. But anyone who examines the aggregate returns that have been earned by companies during the postwar years will discover something extraordinary: the returns on equity have in fact not varied much at all.

The coupon is sticky

In the first 10 years after the war—the decade ending in 1955—the Dow Jones Industrials had an average annual return on year-end equity of 12.8 percent. In the second decade the figure was 10.1 percent. In the third decade it was 10.9 percent. Data for a larger universe, the Fortune 500 (whose history goes back only to the mid-1950s), indicate somewhat similar results: 11.2 percent in the decade ending in 1965, 11.8 percent in the decade through 1975. The figures for a few exceptional years have been substantially higher (the high for the 500 was 14.1 percent in 1974) or lower (9.5 percent in 1958 and 1970), but over the years, and in the aggregate, the return on book value tends to keep coming back to a level around 12 percent. It shows no signs of exceeding that level significantly in inflationary years (or in years of stable prices, for that matter).

For the moment, let's think of those companies, not as listed stocks, but as productive enterprises. Let's also assume that the owners of those enterprises had acquired them at book value. In that case, their own return would have been around 12 percent too. And because the return has been so consistent, it seems reasonable to think of it as an "equity coupon."

In the real world, of course, investors in stocks don't just buy and hold. Instead, many try to outwit their fellow investors in order to maximize their own proportions of corporate earnings. This thrashing about, obviously fruitless in aggregate, has no impact on the equity coupon but reduces the investor's portion of it, because he incurs substantial frictional costs, such as advisory fees and brokerage charges. Throw in an active options market, which adds nothing to

24

the productivity of American enterprise but requires a cast of thousands to man the casino, and frictional costs rise further.

Stocks are perpetual

It is also true that in the real world investors in stocks don't usually get to buy at book value. Sometimes they have been able to buy in below book; usually, however, they've had to pay more than book, and when that happens there is further pressure on that 12 percent. I'll talk more about these relationships later. Meanwhile, let's focus on the main point: *as inflation has increased, the return on equity capital has not.* Essentially, those who buy equities receive securities with an underlying fixed return—just like those who buy bonds.

Of course, there are some important differences between the bond and stock forms. For openers, bonds eventually come due. It may require a long wait, but eventually the bond investor gets to renegotiate the terms of his contract. If current and prospective rates of inflation make his old coupon look inadequate, he can refuse to play further unless coupons currently being offered rekindle his interest. Something of this sort has been going on in recent years.

Stocks, on the other hand, are perpetual. They have a maturity date of infinity. Investors in stocks are stuck with whatever return corporate America happens to earn. If corporate America is destined to earn 12 percent, then that is the level investors must learn to live with. As a group, stock investors can neither opt out nor renegotiate. In the aggregate, their commitment is actually increasing. Individual companies can be sold or liquidated, and corporations can repurchase their own shares; on balance, however, new equity flotations and retained earnings guarantee that the equity capital locked up in the corporate system will increase.

So, score one for the bond form. Bond coupons eventually will be renegotiated; equity "coupons" won't. It is true, of

25

course, that for a long time a 12 percent coupon did not appear in need of a whole lot of correction.

The bondholder gets it in cash

There is another major difference between the garden variety of bond and our new, exotic 12 percent "equity bond" that comes to the Wall Street costume ball dressed in a stock certificate.

In the usual case, a bond investor receives his entire coupon in cash and is left to reinvest it as best he can. Our stock investor's equity coupon, in contrast, is partially retained by the company and is reinvested at whatever rates the company happens to be earning. In other words, going back to our corporate universe, part of the 12 percent earned annually is paid out in dividends and the balance is put right back into the universe to earn 12 percent also.

The good old days

This characteristic of stocks—the reinvestment of part of the coupon—can be good or bad news, depending on the relative attractiveness of that 12 percent. The news was very good indeed in the 1950s and early 1960s. With bonds yielding only 3 or 4 percent, the right to reinvest automatically a portion of the equity coupon at 12 percent was of enormous value. Note that investors could not just invest their own money and get that 12 percent return. Stock prices in this period ranged far above book value, and investors were prevented by the premium prices they had to pay from directly extracting out of the underlying corporate universe whatever rate that universe was earning. You can't pay far above par for a 12 percent bond and earn 12 percent for yourself.

But on their retained earnings, investors *could* earn 12 percent. In effect, earnings retention allowed investors to buy at book value part of an enterprise that, in the economic

26

environment then existing, was worth a great deal more than book value.

It was a situation that left very little to be said for cash dividends and a lot to be said for earnings retention. Indeed, the more money that investors thought likely to be reinvested at the 12 percent rate, the more valuable they considered their reinvestment privilege and the more they were willing to pay for it. In the early 1960s, investors eagerly paid top-scale prices for electric utilities situated in growth areas, knowing that these companies had the ability to reinvest very large proportions of their earnings. Utilities whose operating environment dictated a larger cash payout rated lower prices.

If, during this period, a high-grade, noncallable, long-term bond with a 12 percent coupon had existed, it would have sold far above par. And if it were a bond with a further unusual characteristic—which was that most of the coupon payments could be automatically reinvested at par in similar bonds—the issue would have commanded an even greater premium. In essence, growth stocks retaining most of their earnings represented just such a security. When their reinvestment rate on the added equity capital was 12 percent while interest rates generally were around 4 percent, investors became very happy—and, of course, they paid happy prices.

Heading for the exits

Looking back, stock investors can think of themselves in the 1946-66 period as having been ladled a truly bountiful triple dip. First, they were the beneficiaries of an underlying corporate return on equity that was far above prevailing interest rates. Second, a significant portion of that return was reinvested for them at rates that were otherwise unattainable. And third, they were afforded an escalating appraisal of underlying equity capital as the first two benefits became widely recognized. This third dip meant that, on top of the basic 12 percent or so earned by corporations on their equity capital, investors were receiving a bonus as the Dow Jones Industrials increased in price from 133 percent of book value in 1946 to 220 percent in 1966. Such a marking-up process temporarily allowed investors to achieve a return that exceeded the inherent earning power of the enterprises in which they had invested.

This heaven-on-earth situation finally was "discovered" in the mid-1960s by many major investing institutions. But just as these financial elephants began trampling on one another in their rush to equities, we entered an era of accelerating inflation and higher interest rates. Quite logically, the marking-up process began to reverse itself. Rising interest rates ruthlessly reduced the value of all existing fixed-coupon investments. And as long-term corporate bond rates began moving up (eventually reaching the 10 percent area), both the equity return of 12 percent and the reinvestment "privilege" began to look different.

Stocks are quite properly thought of as riskier than bonds. While that equity coupon is more or less fixed over periods of time, it does fluctuate somewhat from year to year. Investors' attitudes about the future can be affected substantially, although frequently erroneously, by those yearly changes. Stocks are also riskier because they come equipped with infinite maturities. (Even your friendly broker wouldn't have the nerve to peddle a 100-year bond, if he had any available, as "safe.") Because of the additional risk, the natural reaction of investors is to expect an equity return that is comfortably above the bond return—and 12 percent on equity versus, say, 10 percent on bonds issued by the same corporate universe does not seem to qualify as comfortable. As the spread narrows, equity investors start looking for the exits.

But, of course, as a group they can't get out. All they can achieve is a lot of movement, substantial frictional costs, and a new, much lower level of valuation, reflecting the lessened attractiveness of the 12 percent equity coupon under inflationary conditions. Bond investors have had a succession of

28

shocks over the past decade in the course of discovering that there is no magic attached to any given coupon level: at 6 percent, or 8 percent, or 10 percent, bonds can still collapse in price. Stock investors, who are in general not aware that they too have a "coupon," are still receiving their education on this point.

Five ways to improve earnings

Must we really view that 12 percent equity coupon as immutable? Is there any law that says the corporate return on equity capital cannot adjust itself upward in response to a permanently higher average rate of inflation?

There is no such law, of course. On the other hand, corporate America cannot increase earnings by desire or decree. To raise that return on equity, corporations would need at least one of the following: (1) an increase in turnover, i.e., in the ratio between sales and total assets employed in the business; (2) cheaper leverage; (3) more leverage; (4) lower income taxes; (5) wider operating margins on sales.

And that's it. There simply are no other ways to increase returns on common equity. Let's see what can be done with these.

We'll begin with *turnover*. The three major categories of assets we have to think about for this exercise are accounts receivable, inventories, and fixed assets such as plants and machinery.

Accounts receivable go up proportionally as sales go up, whether the increase in dollar sales is produced by more physical volume or by inflation. No room for improvement here.

With inventories the situation is not quite so simple. Over the long term, the trend in unit inventories may be expected to follow the trend in unit sales. Over the short term, however, the physical turnover rate may bob around because of special influences—e.g., cost expectations or bottlenecks.

The use of last-in, first-out (LIFO) inventory-valuation

methods serves to increase the reported turnover rate during inflationary times. When dollar sales are rising because of inflation, inventory valuations of a LIFO company either will remain level (if unit sales are not rising) or will trail the rise in dollar sales (if unit sales are rising). In either case, dollar turnover will increase.

During the early 1970s there was a pronounced swing by corporations toward LIFO accounting (which has the effect of lowering a company's reported earnings and tax bills). The trend now seems to have slowed. Still, the existence of a lot of LIFO companies, plus the likelihood that some others will join the crowd, ensures some further increase in the reported turnover of inventory.

The gains are apt to be modest

In the case of fixed assets, any rise in the inflation rate, assuming it affects all products equally, will initially have the effect of increasing turnover. That is true because sales will immediately reflect the new price level, while the fixed-asset account will reflect the change only gradually, i.e., as existing assets are retired and replaced at the new prices. Obviously, the more slowly a company goes about this replacement process, the more the turnover ratio will rise. The action stops, however, when a replacement cycle is completed. Assuming a constant rate of inflation, sales and fixed assets will then begin to rise in concert at the rate of inflation.

To sum up, inflation will produce some gains in turnover ratios. Some improvement would be certain because of LIFO, and some would be possible (if inflation accelerates) because of sales rising more rapidly than fixed assets. But the gains are apt to be modest and not of a magnitude to produce substantial improvement in returns on equity capital. During the decade ending in 1975, despite generally accelerating inflation and the extensive use of LIFO accounting, the turnover ratio of the Fortune 500 went only from 1.18:1 to 1.29:1.

30

Cheaper leverage? Not likely. High rates of inflation generally cause borrowing to become dearer, not cheaper. Galloping rates of inflation create galloping capital needs; and lenders, as they become increasingly distrustful of long-term contracts, become more demanding. But even if there is no further rise in interest rates, leverage will be getting more expensive because the average cost of the debt now on corporate books is less than would be the cost of replacing it. And replacement will be required as the existing debt matures. Overall, then, future changes in the cost of leverage seem likely to have a mildly depressing effect on the return on equity.

More leverage? American business already has fired many, if not most, of the more-leverage bullets once available to it. Proof of that proposition can be seen in some other Fortune 500 statistics: in the 20 years ending in 1975, stockholders' equity as a percentage of total assets declined for the 500 from 63 percent to just under 50 percent. In other words, each dollar of equity capital is now leveraged much more heavily than it used to be.

What the lenders learned

An irony of inflation-induced financial requirements is that the highly profitable companies—generally the best credits—require relatively little debt capital. But the laggards in profitability never can get enough. Lenders understand this problem much better than they did a decade ago—and are correspondingly less willing to let capital-hungry, low-profitability enterprises leverage themselves to the sky.

Nevertheless, given inflationary conditions, many corporations seem sure in the future to turn to still more leverage as a means of shoring up equity returns. Their managements will make that move because they will need enormous amounts of capital—often merely to do the same physical volume of business—and will wish to get it without cutting dividends or making equity offerings that, because of inflation, are not apt to shape up as attractive. Their natural response will be to heap on debt, almost regardless of cost. They will tend to behave like those utility companies that argued over an eighth of a point in the 1960s and were grateful to find 12 percent debt financing in 1974.

Added debt at present interest rates, however, will do less for equity returns than did added debt at 4 percent rates in the early 1960s. There is also the problem that higher debt ratios cause credit ratings to be lowered, creating a further rise in interest costs.

So that is another way, to be added to those already discussed, in which the cost of leverage will be rising. In total, the higher costs of leverage are likely to offset the benefits of greater leverage.

Besides, there is already far more debt in corporate America than is conveyed by conventional balance sheets. Many companies have massive pension obligations geared to whatever pay levels will be in effect when present workers retire. At the low inflation rates of 1955-65, the liabilities arising from such plans were reasonably predictable. Today, nobody can really know the company's ultimate obligation. But if the inflation rate averages 7 percent in the future, a 25-year-old employee who is now earning $12,000, and whose raises do no more than match increases in living costs, will be making $180,000 when he retires at 65.

Of course, there is a marvelously precise figure in many annual reports each year, purporting to be the unfunded pension liability. If that figure were really believable, a corporation could simply ante up that sum, add to it the existing pension fund assets, turn the total amount over to an insurance company, and have it assume all the corporation's present pension liabilities. In the real world, alas, it is impossible to find an insurance company willing even to listen to such a deal.

Virtually every corporate treasurer in America would recoil at the idea of issuing a "cost-of-living" bond—a noncallable obligation with coupons tied to a price index. But through the private pension system, corporate America has in fact taken on a fantastic amount of debt that is the equivalent of such a bond.

More leverage, whether through conventional debt or unbooked and indexed "pension debt," should be viewed with skepticism by shareholders. A 12 percent return from an enterprise that is debt-free is far superior to the same return achieved by a business hocked to its eyeballs. Which means that today's 12 percent equity returns may well be less valuable than the 12 percent returns of 20 years ago.

More fun in New York

Lower corporate income taxes seem unlikely. Investors in American corporations already own what might be thought of as a class D stock. The class A, B, and C stocks are represented by the income tax claims of the federal, state, and municipal governments. It is true that these "investors" have no claim on the corporation's assets; however, they get a major share of the earnings, including earnings generated by the equity buildup resulting from retention of part of the earnings owned by the class D shareholders.

A further charming characteristic of these wonderful class A, B, and C stocks is that their share of the corporation's earnings can be increased immediately, abundantly, and without payment by the unilateral vote of any one of the "stockholder" classes, e.g., by congressional action in the case of class A. To add to the fun, one of the classes will sometimes vote to increase its ownership share in the business retroactively—as companies operating in New York discovered to their dismay in 1975. Whenever the class A, B, or C "stockholders" vote themselves a larger share of the business, the portion remaining for class D—that's the one held by the ordinary investor—declines.

Looking ahead, it seems unwise to assume that those who

control the A, B, and C shares will vote to reduce their own take over the long run. The class D shares probably will have to struggle to hold their own.

Bad news from the FTC

The last of our five possible sources of increased returns on equity is *wider operating margins on sales.* Here is where some optimists would hope to achieve major gains. There is no proof that they are wrong. But there are only 100 cents in the sales dollar and a lot of demands on that dollar before we get down to the residual, pretax profits. The major claimants are labor, raw materials, energy, and various nonincome taxes. The relative importance of these costs hardly seems likely to decline during an age of inflation.

Recent statistical evidence, furthermore, does not inspire confidence in the proposition that margins will widen in a period of inflation. In the decade ending in 1965, a period of relatively low inflation, the universe of manufacturing companies reported on quarterly by the Federal Trade Commission had an average annual pretax margin on sales of 8.6 percent. In the decade ending in 1975, the average margin was 8 percent. Margins were down, in other words, despite a very considerable increase in the inflation rate.

If business were able to base its prices on replacement costs, margins would widen in inflationary periods. But the simple fact is that most large businesses, despite a widespread belief in their market power, just don't manage to pull it off. Replacement cost accounting almost always shows that corporate earnings have declined significantly in the past decade. If such major industries as oil, steel, and aluminum really have the oligopolistic muscle imputed to them, one can only conclude that their pricing policies have been remarkably restrained.

There you have the complete lineup: five factors that can improve returns on common equity, none of which, by my analysis, are likely to take us very far in that direction in

34

periods of high inflation. You may have emerged from this exercise more optimistic than I am. But remember, returns in the 12 percent area have been with us a long time.

The investor's equation

Even if you agree that the 12 percent equity coupon is more or less immutable, you still may hope to do well with it in the years ahead. It's conceivable that you will. After all, a lot of investors did well with it for a long time. But your future results will be governed by three variables: the relationship between book value and market value, the tax rate, and the inflation rate.

Let's wade through a little arithmetic about book and market value. When stocks consistently sell at book value, it's all very simple. If a stock has a book value of $100 and also an average market value of $100, 12 percent earnings by business will produce a 12 percent return for the investor (less those frictional costs, which we'll ignore for the moment). If the payout ratio is 50 percent, our investor will get $6 via dividends and a further $6 from the increase in the book value of the business, which will, of course, be reflected in the market value of his holdings.

If the stock sold at 150 percent of book value, the picture would change. The investor would receive the same $6 cash dividend, but it would now represent only a 4 percent return on his $150 cost. The book value of the business would still increase by 6 percent (to $106), and the market value of the investor's holdings, valued consistently at 150 percent of book value, would similarly increase by 6 percent (to $159). But the investor's total return, i.e., from appreciation plus dividends, would be only 10 percent versus the underlying 12 percent earned by the business.

When the investor buys in below book value, the process is reversed. For example, if the stock sells at 80 percent of book value, the same earnings and payout assumptions would yield 7.5 percent from dividends ($6 on an $80 price) and 6 percent from appreciation—a total return of 13.5 percent. In other words, you do better by buying at a discount rather than a premium, just as common sense would suggest.

During the postwar years, the market value of the Dow Jones Industrials has been as low as 84 percent of book value (in 1974) and as high as 232 percent (in 1965); most of the time the ratio has been well over 100 percent. (In early 1977 it was around 110 percent.) Let's assume that in the future the ratio will be something close to 100 percent—meaning that investors in stocks could earn the full 12 percent. At least, they could earn that figure before taxes and before inflation.

Seven percent after taxes

How large a bite might taxes take out of the 12 percent? For individual investors, it seems reasonable to assume that federal, state, and local income taxes will average perhaps 50 percent on dividends and 30 percent on capital gains. A majority of investors may have marginal rates somewhat below these, but many with larger holdings will experience substantially higher rates. Under 1977 tax laws, a high-income investor in a heavily taxed city could have a marginal rate on capital gains as high as 56 percent.

So let's use 50 percent and 30 percent as representative for individual investors. Let's also assume, in line with recent experience, that corporations earning 12 percent on equity pay out 5 percent in cash dividends (2.5 percent after tax) and retain 7 percent, with those retained earnings producing a corresponding market-value growth (4.9 percent after the 30 percent tax). The aftertax return, then, would be 7.4 percent. Probably this should be rounded down to about 7 percent to allow for frictional costs. To push our stocks-as-disguised-bonds thesis one notch further, then, stocks might be regarded as the equivalent, for individuals, of 7 percent tax-exempt perpetual bonds.

36

The number nobody knows

Which brings us to the crucial question—the inflation rate. No one knows the answer on this one—including the politicians, economists, and Establishment pundits, who felt, a few years back, that with slight nudges here and there unemployment and inflation rates would respond like trained seals.

But many signs seem negative for stable prices: the fact that inflation is now worldwide; the propensity of major groups in our society to utilize their electoral muscle to shift, rather than solve, economic problems; the demonstrated unwillingness to tackle even the most vital problems (e.g., energy and nuclear proliferation) if they can be postponed; and a political system that rewards legislators with reelection if their actions appear to produce short-term benefits even though their ultimate imprint will be to compound long-term pain.

Most of those in political office, quite understandably, are firmly against inflation and firmly in favor of policies producing it. (This schizophrenia hasn't caused them to lose touch with reality, however; congressmen have made sure that *their* pensions—unlike practically all granted in the private sector—are indexed to cost-of-living changes *after* retirement.)

Discussions regarding future inflation rates usually probe the subtleties of monetary and fiscal policies. These are important variables in determining the outcome of any specific inflationary equation. But, at the source, peacetime inflation is a political problem, not an economic problem. Human behavior, not monetary behavior, is the key. And when very human politicians choose between the next election and the next generation, it's clear what usually happens.

Such broad generalizations do not produce precise numbers. However, it seems quite possible to me that inflation rates will average 7 percent in future years. I hope this forecast proves to be wrong. And it may well be. Forecasts usually tell us more of the forecaster than of the future. You are free to factor your own inflation rate into the investor's equation. But if you foresee a rate averaging 2 percent or 3 percent, you are wearing different glasses than I am.

So there we are: 12 percent before taxes and inflation; 7 percent after taxes and before inflation; and maybe 0 percent after taxes and inflation. It hardly sounds like a formula that will keep all those cattle stampeding on TV.

As a common stockholder you will have more dollars, but you may have no more purchasing power. Out with Ben Franklin ("a penny saved is a penny earned") and in with Milton Friedman ("a man might as well consume his capital as invest it").

What widows don't notice

The arithmetic makes it plain that inflation is a far more devastating tax than anything that has been enacted by our legislators. The inflation tax has a fantastic ability to simply consume capital. It makes no difference to a widow with her savings in a 5 percent passbook account whether she pays 100 percent income tax on her interest income during a period of zero inflation, or pays *no* income taxes during years of 5 percent inflation. Either way, she is "taxed" in a manner that leaves her no real income whatsoever. Any money she spends comes right out of capital. She would find outrageous a 120 percent income tax, but doesn't seem to notice that 6 percent inflation is the economic equivalent.

If my inflation assumption is close to correct, disappointing results will occur not because the market falls, but in spite of the fact that the market rises. At around 920 early in 1977, the Dow was up 55 points from where it was 10 years ago. But adjusted for inflation, the Dow is down almost 345 points—from 865 to 520. And about half of the earnings of the Dow had to be withheld from their owners and reinvested in order to achieve even that result.

In the next 10 years the Dow would be doubled just by a combination of the 12 percent equity coupon, a 40 percent

38

payout ratio, and the present 110 percent ratio of market to book value. And with 7 percent inflation, investors who sold at 1,800 would still be considerably worse off than they are today after paying their capital gains taxes.

I can almost hear the reaction of some investors to these downbeat thoughts. It will be to assume that, whatever the difficulties presented by the new investment era, they will somehow contrive to turn in superior results for themselves. Their success is most unlikely. And, in aggregate, of course, impossible. If you feel you can dance in and out of securities in a way that defeats the inflation tax, I would like to be your broker—but not your partner.

Even the so-called tax-exempt investors, such as pension funds and college endowment funds, do not escape the inflation tax. If my assumption of a 7 percent inflation rate is correct, a college treasurer should regard the first 7 percent earned each year merely as a replenishment of purchasing power. Endowment funds are earning *nothing* until they have outpaced the inflation treadmill. At 7 percent inflation and, say, overall investment returns of 8 percent, these institutions, which believe they are tax exempt, are in fact paying "income taxes" of 87½ percent.

The social equation

Unfortunately, the major problems from high inflation rates flow not to investors but to society as a whole. Investment income is a small portion of national income, and if per capita real income could grow at a healthy rate alongside zero real investment returns, social justice might well be advanced.

A market economy creates some lopsided payoffs to participants. The right endowment of vocal cords, anatomical structure, physical strength, or mental powers can produce enormous piles of claim checks (stocks, bonds, and other forms of capital) on future national output. Proper selection of ancestors similarly can result in lifetime supplies of such tickets upon birth. If zero real investment returns diverted a bit greater portion of the national output from such stockholders to equally worthy and hardworking citizens lacking jackpot-producing talents, it would seem unlikely to pose such an insult to an equitable world as to risk divine intervention.

But the potential for real improvement in the welfare of workers at the expense of affluent stockholders is not significant. Employee compensation already totals 28 times the amount paid out in dividends, and a lot of those dividends now go to pension funds, nonprofit institutions such as universities, and individual stockholders who are not affluent. Under these circumstances, if we now shifted *all* dividends of wealthy stockholders into wages—something we could do only once, like killing a cow (or, if you prefer, a pig)—we would increase real wages by less than we used to obtain from one year's growth of the economy.

The Russians understand it too

Therefore, diminishment of the affluent, through the impact of inflation on their investments, will not even provide material *short-term* aid to those who are not affluent. Their economic well-being will rise or fall with the general effects of inflation on the economy. And those effects are not likely to be good.

Large gains in real capital, invested in modern production facilities, are required to produce large gains in economic well-being. Great labor availability, great consumer wants, and great government promises will lead to nothing but great frustration without continuous creation and employment of expensive new capital assets throughout industry. That's an equation understood by Russians as well as Rockefellers. And it's one that has been applied with stunning success in West Germany and Japan. High capital accumulation rates have enabled those countries to achieve gains in living standards at rates far exceeding ours, even though we have enjoyed much the superior position in energy.

To understand the impact of inflation upon real capital accumulation, a little math is required. Come back for a moment to that 12 percent return on equity capital. Such earnings are stated after depreciation, which presumably will allow replacement of present productive capacity—*if* that plant and equipment can be purchased in the future at prices similar to their original cost.

The way it was

Let's assume that about half of earnings are paid out in dividends, leaving 6 percent of equity capital available to finance future growth. If inflation is low—say, 2 percent—a large portion of that growth can be real growth in physical output. For under these conditions, 2 percent more will have to be invested in receivables, inventories, and fixed assets next year just to duplicate this year's physical output—leaving 4 percent for investment in assets to produce more physical goods. The 2 percent finances illusory dollar growth reflecting inflation, and the remaining 4 percent finances real growth. If population growth is 1 percent, the 4 percent gain in real output translates into a 3 percent gain in real per capita net income. That, very roughly, is what used to happen in our economy.

Now move the inflation rate to 7 percent and compute what is left for real growth after the financing of the mandatory inflation component. The answer is nothing—if dividend policies and leverage ratios remain unchanged. After half of the 12 percent earnings are paid out, the same 6 percent is left, but it is all conscripted to provide the added dollars needed to transact last year's physical volume of business.

Many companies, faced with no real retained earnings with which to finance physical expansion after normal dividend payments, will improvise. How, they will ask themselves, can we stop or reduce dividends without risking stockholder wrath? I have good news for them: a ready-made set of blueprints is available.

In recent years the electric utility industry has had little or no dividend-paying capacity. Or, rather, it has had the power to pay dividends *if* investors agree to buy stock from them. In 1975 electric utilities paid common dividends of $3.3 billion and asked investors to return $3.4 billion. Of course, they mixed in a little solicit-Peter-to-pay-Paul technique so as not to acquire a Con Ed reputation. Con Ed, you will remember, was unwise enough in 1974 to simply tell its shareholders it didn't have the money to pay the dividend. Candor was rewarded with calamity in the marketplace.

The more sophisticated utility maintains—perhaps increases—the quarterly dividend and then asks shareholders (either old or new) to mail back the money. In other words, the company issues new stock. This procedure diverts massive amounts of capital to the tax collector and substantial sums to underwriters. Everyone, however, seems to remain in good spirits (particularly the underwriters).

More joy at AT&T

Encouraged by such success, some utilities have devised a further shortcut. In this case, the company declares the dividend, the shareholder pays the tax, and—presto—more shares are issued. No cash changes hands, although the IRS, spoilsport as always, persists in treating the transaction as if it had.

AT&T, for example, instituted a dividend reinvestment program in 1973. This company, in fairness, must be described as very stockholder-minded, and its adoption of this program, considering the folkways of finance, must be regarded as totally understandable. But the substance of the program is out of *Alice in Wonderland.*

In 1976 AT&T paid $2.3 billion in cash dividends to about 2.9 million owners of its common stock. At the end of the year, 648,000 holders (up from 601,000 the previous year) reinvested $432 million (up from $327 million) in additional shares supplied directly by the company.

Just for fun, let's assume that all AT&T shareholders ultimately sign up for this program. In that case, no cash at all would be mailed to shareholders—just as when Con Ed passed a dividend. However, each of the 2.9 million owners would be notified that he should pay income taxes on his share of the retained earnings that had that year been called a "dividend." Assuming that "dividends" totaled $2.3 billion, as in 1976, and that shareholders paid an average tax of 30 percent on these, they would end up, courtesy of this marvelous plan, paying nearly $700 million to the IRS. Imagine the joy of shareholders, in such circumstances, if the directors were then to double the dividend.

The government will try to do it

We can expect to see more use of disguised payout reductions as business struggles with the problem of real capital accumulation. But throttling back shareholders somewhat will not entirely solve the problem. A combination of 7 percent inflation and 12 percent returns will reduce the stream of corporate capital available to finance real growth.

And so, as conventional private capital accumulation methods falter under inflation, our government will increasingly attempt to influence capital flows to industry, either unsuccessfully as in England or successfully as in Japan. The necessary cultural and historical underpinning for a Japanese-style enthusiastic partnership of government, business, and labor seems lacking here. If we are lucky, we will avoid following the English path, where all segments fight over division of the pie rather than pool their energies to enlarge it.

On balance, however, it seems likely that we will hear a great deal more as the years unfold about underinvestment, stagflation, and the failures of the private sector to fulfill needs.

3

Stocks Are Not an Inflation Hedge

by

Richard W. Kopcke

STOCKS ARE NOT AN INFLATION HEDGE
by Richard W. Kopcke

During the 1960s investors generally believed that common stocks offered the opportunity to share in America's growth. Stockholders would receive not only dividends from the profits of corporate business but also capital gains from reinvested earnings. Perhaps the most attractive attribute of common stocks—especially during the late 1960s—was their image as an inflation hedge. When prices rise, the purchasing power of money, bills, and bonds declines. Stock prices, however, would rise in step with the prices of goods and services. After all, the value of shares ought to reflect both the value of corporate assets—land, buildings, equipment, and inventories—and the value of prospective corporate profits. When the prices of goods and services rose, would not the value of assets and the flow of profits also rise, thereby increasing stock prices?

Fifteen years ago this logic sounded almost too good to be true. Some of us know better today. Since the late 1960s and early 1970s, both the Standard & Poor's index of 500 common stock prices and the Dow Jones Industrials index have declined more than 40 percent relative to the prices of goods and services produced by U.S. businesses. While prices generally doubled from 1969 to 1980, equity values have hardly changed. Even the 1980 bull market accomplished little more than the restoration of the real stock prices that prevailed in 1978 and 1979.

What went wrong?

Some would have us believe the market does not know how to value corporate assets, so that those who buy and hold today must surely be rewarded handsomely once others become enlightened. Delusions may persist for an hour, perhaps days, or even a few months, but 10 years of bungling is difficult to believe.

I do not believe that stock prices have become unhinged from the value of underlying corporate earnings or the value of corporate assets. The reasons real stock prices have fallen so drastically are many, and they raise many complicated issues, but I want to draw your attention to what I consider the foremost reason for the declining purchasing power of equities.[1] I believe that those who buy and sell stocks pay close attention to the prospective profits of corporate business when valuing equities, and during the past 10 years those profits have been depressed because of our unexpected and persistently high rate of inflation.

My principal conclusion is that stocks are a perverse inflation hedge. This does not mean that equities are hazardous to your health. Stocks are priced today to yield very lucrative returns. The prospective returns have to be good, however, to compensate stockholders for the risk they bear because equities are a perverse inflation hedge. When the rate of inflation unexpectedly increases, real stock prices will fall. Conversely, when the rate of inflation unexpectedly drops, real stock prices will rise. So if one does not mind bearing some risk—especially the risk that the inflation rate may be higher than we expect during the 1980s—stocks are a good investment. If one seeks an inflation hedge, stocks are generally poor investments. My conclusion rests on the observation that rising inflation rates tend to depress corporate earnings after taxes, and thereby stock prices.

Inflation and taxes

Common stock represents an ownership claim on the prospective aftertax earnings commanded by corporate assets. Even though the prices of goods and services have generally

---

[1] See also Richard W. Kopcke, "Are Stocks a Bargain?" *New England Economic Review*, May-June 1979; and "Primer on Stock Prices and Inflation," *New England Economic Review*, 1981.

risen during the past 10 years, suggesting that corporate earnings and equity values might also rise, the real income tax rate, or the effective income tax rate, on those corporate profits has also increased fast enough to depress aftertax earnings on corporate assets financed by equity.

Because this higher corporate income tax rate has been caused by the unexpectedly high inflation rate of the 1970s, the real tax burden on corporate profits has risen with inflation. Accordingly, real stock prices tend to fall when the inflation rate rises. Those who would argue that real stock prices have been depressed because investor risk premiums have increased with the inflation rate must also rest their arguments on a similar link between inflation and corporate income taxation. If real aftertax profits were not depressed when inflation unexpectedly rose, why should the risk premium for equity have increased? Indeed, the flight from bonds might even depress equity's risk premium under these circumstances.

Reported profits rest on accounting principles that presume prices are reasonably stable from year to year. For instance, depreciation allowances are tied to the original acquisition prices of plant and equipment. Accordingly, capital consumption allowances reflect asset prices that may be significantly out of date after a period of rising prices. The cost of doing business is therefore understated, profits are overstated, and business income tax liabilities increase relative to actual earnings. The cost of production is also linked to the purchase prices of raw materials and intermediate products. Due to the lags between product acquisition, production, and sales, products are held in process or inventory for lengthy periods before being sold. Consequently, the cost of the materials behind current sales may also be understated during periods of inflation, creating *inventory holding gains.* These inventory profits are included in reported income, and they are taxed accordingly. Therefore, the effective corporate income tax rate on operating income, which excludes inventory and depreciation profits, rises with the inflation rate.

Figure 3-1 shows that although corporate income taxes were only 38 percent of reported profits in 1980, these taxes were 60 percent of operating income. Inflation, according to this standard, has elevated recent corporate tax liabilities more than 50 percent.

Figure 3-1: Income tax liability of nonfinancial corporations as a percentage of profits

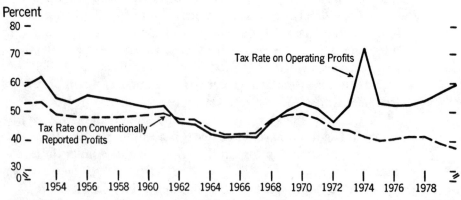

Note: The tax rate on conventionally reported profits equals the profits tax liability divided by profits before tax. The tax rate on operating profits equals the profits tax liability divided by corporate profits with inventory valuation and capital consumption adjustments.

Source: Department of Commerce, *Survey of Current Business*, National Income and Product Accounts, table 1.15. The data for the fourth quarter of 1980 are estimates.

Not only does the effective corporate income tax rate rise with inflation, but the effective personal income tax rate on corporate earnings rises as well. Because a portion of corporate earnings is reinvested in the firm, stockholders receive these retained earnings, not as dividends, but as capital gains on existing equity. When the accumulated capital gains are redeemed by stockholders selling equity, this deferred income is taxed according to the income tax rates on personal capital gains. Investors may also expect equity values to rise with the prices of goods and services, but in this case the increasing stock prices, which only maintain stockholders' purchasing power, are also subject to capital gains taxes, even though

50

these capital gains do not represent deferred income. Equity values must fall relative to dividends and corporate earnings with the first signs of higher inflation to raise the nominal yield on stocks enough to compensate new investors for the higher real tax burden due to this taxation of capital gains caused by inflation. Consequently, stock prices are lower than they would have been if the inflation-induced capital gains had not been taxed. The higher the expected rate of inflation, the lower stock price-earnings ratios must fall to sustain stockholders' real compensation.

To recapitulate. An unexpected increase in the inflation rate would tend to depress the aftertax earnings on capital, thereby depressing the value of corporate assets to potential owners. Accordingly, real stock prices tend to fall. Of course, stock prices would not fall to zero. Once assets and equity values have been marked down sufficiently, the return on assets and equity would again become competitive. Barring any unexpected increases in the inflation rate, stocks would therefore provide investors with attractive returns, including capital gains. With capital gains taxes, though, real stock prices must initially drop even lower to provide stockholders with competitive returns.

Inflation, purchasing power gains on debt, and purchasing power losses on pension fund reserves

However businesses measure profits or report earnings, unexpectedly higher rates of inflation must increase the income tax burdens on stockholders. Unless businesses can increase their prices faster than the general rate of inflation (by definition, I am not sure that is possible), a rising tax burden must reduce prospective aftertax earnings.

Some would say this argument is fine as far as it goes, but they would remind me that debtors benefit during periods of inflation and that many corporate assets are financed by debt. I accept this point. Nevertheless, the return to all capital—both bond financed and stock financed—has declined because of the increased tax burden on corporate profits during the past 10 years.[2] Therefore, even if we were to account correctly for the transfer of wealth from bondholders to stockholders due to inflation, the pie that both bondholders and stockholders must share is shrinking. Figure 3-2

Figure 3-2: Aftertax rate of return on capital for nonfinancial corporations

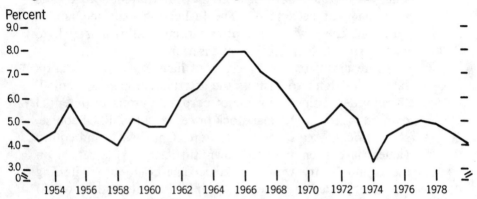

Note: The rate of return equals nonfinancial corporate profits with inventory valuation and capital consumption adjustments, less profits tax liability, plus net interest, divided by the current replacement value of nonfinancial assets.

shows that the real return on all corporate capital has declined from nearly 8 percent in the mid-1960s to 5 percent in the late 1970s. The rising tax burden on profits has accounted for half of this slump. Prospective profits must be squeezed unless we can depend upon creditors becoming philanthropists or patsies. (It is true that the difference between corporate tax rates and the tax rates of bondholders may provide stockholders with some relief, but this assistance is not great enough to offset the increasing income tax burden. See my "Why Interest Rates Are So Low," *New England Economic Review,* July-August 1980.)

---

[2] I discussed this in "The Decline in Corporate Profitability," *New England Economic Review,* May-June 1978.

Unexpected inflation can diminish the burden of debt obligations. To the extent that plant, equipment, and other nonfinancial assets are financed with debt, whose value declines relative to these capital assets due to its fixed nominal liability, holding gains accrue to stockholders—that is, outstanding debt obligations may be satisfied by sacrificing a smaller proportion of revenue than had been expected. Even though unexpected inflation increases a corporation's tax liability relative to its operating income, the same inflation will also reduce the relative burden of outstanding commitments to creditors, providing some compensation for the higher tax rate. Once the debt is retired, however, the real burden of debt service charges will be restored.

A widely expected increase in the inflation rate does not provide stockholders with similar benefits. In this case, potential creditors and stockholders alike recognize that inflation reduces the real value of debt contracts. Accordingly, the creditors will seek, and businesses will pay, higher yields on debt to compensate for the declining purchasing power on loans. In this case, if one believes profits have declined because he has ignored the holding gains on debt that offset the higher inflation premium in debt yields, then he has made a mistake.

When inflation unexpectedly rises, debt service charges do not embody the full inflation premium. Until the debt is rolled over, adding purchasing power gains on net financial liabilities to corporate profits may make profits look attractive. Upon refinancing, however, the new debt yields will increase financing costs and offset the purchasing power gains on debt, thereby depressing profits. Ultimately, unexpectedly high inflation rates only offer stockholders the opportunity to pay more taxes.

During periods of inflation stockholders may also experience holding losses on existing capital assets. From 1968 to 1978 neither the pretax return per unit of corporate capital nor the aftertax return on all corporate capital—both bond and equity financed—has increased as rapidly as the price of *new* capital goods, so the inflation rate has over-stated the holding gains stockholders have received by financing real assets with debt. Compared to profits or the market value of corporate assets, the real burden of obligations to creditors has declined more slowly than the inflation rate might suggest—the purchasing power gains on debt have been offset to a degree by substantial purchasing power losses on existing capital.

In Figure 3-3, I have plotted three measure of the rate of return on stockholders' equity for nonfinancial corporations. The dotted line represents corporate profits after taxes, less depreciation and inventory profits (operating income),

Figure 3-3: Aftertax returns on stockholders' equity

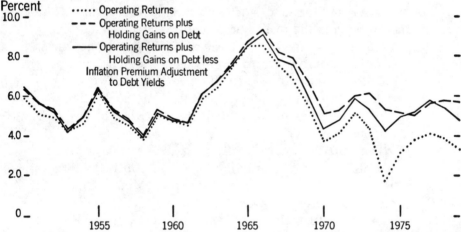

Note: Operating income equals nonfinancial corporate (NFC) profits with inventory valuation and capital consumption adjustments, less profits tax liability. Holding gains on debt equal the fourth-quarter to fourth-quarter rate of change in the deflator for nonfarm business product times average net financial liabilities of NFCs. The inflation premium adjustment equals average long-term liabilities (bonds and mortgages) of NFCs times the aftertax difference between average short-term yields and average outstanding bond yields. Short-term yields are estimated by adding 100 basis points to LIBOR (50 basis points to the Eurodollar rate before 1970); long-term yields are estimated by the gross coupon yields on life insurance company bond portfolios.

Source: Department of Commerce, National Income and, Product Accounts; Board of Governors of the Federal Reserve System, Flow of Funds Accounts, *Balance Sheets for the U. S. Economy,* Salomon Brothers, *An Analytical Records of Yields and Yield Spreads;* and American Council of Life Insurance.

divided by the value of corporate assets financed by stockholders. The dashed line describes the return on equity after I have added purchasing power holding gains on debt to operating income. The solid line represents operating income plus holding gains on debt, less the sum of a debt yield adjustment and holding losses on pension fund reserves, all divided by the value of assets financed by equity. If holding gains on debt have elevated corporate earnings, then the best measure of "sustainable earnings" must also consider how much profits will decline once debt service charges rise to cover the inflation premium in debt yields as debt is refinanced and once compensation costs rise to cover purchasing power holding losses on pension fund reserves. According to the solid line in Figure 3-3, the sustainable rate of return on equity capital has dropped approximately 40 percent since the mid-1960s. This is not surprising, given the acute slump in operating income due partly to rising tax liabilities. The decline in real stock prices since the late 1960s, therefore, merely reflects a deterioration in the quality of corporate earnings.

Most of the holding gains on debt, however, are offset by the holding losses of corporate pension plans. Business pension liabilities are linked to wages and salaries earned by employees during their tenure with their firms. To meet these obligations, firms establish pension fund reserves. Though pension fund assets are owned by employees, pension contracts obligate their sponsors to assure that the pension fund will satisfy the liabilities of the plan. Accordingly, stockholder obligations increase whenever the inflation rate unexpectedly rises, because the present value of pension liabilities exceeds accumulated reserves. For example, with a 4 percent inflation rate a typical fully funded pension plan holds assets whose yield is high enough to provide adequate financing for the vested retirement obligations of the firm. Should the inflation rate unexpectedly increase to 8 percent, the future benefits promised by the firm increase substantially—benefits are most commonly linked to an employee's last five years of compensation—but the assets of the plan are now locked into securities with relatively low and inadequate yields. The firm must satisfy this newly created "liability" of the plan, so the annual purchasing power losses on existing pension fund assets are transferred from the plan to stockholders.

The size of pension fund reserves roughly matches long-term corporate debt outstanding, about $600 billion today. So if we consider pension plans and long-term debt positions together, the rise in the expected inflation rate since the 1960s has conferred on equity no net profit from lower real debt burdens. On average, net holding gains on bonds cannot provide any improvement in real equity values. The purchasing power loss on pension fund reserves roughly matches any purchasing power gain on debt. Of course, firms carrying heavier than average debt loads and modest pension obligations would benefit from inflation, whereas some manufacturing businesses with relatively light debt loads and substantial pension commitments would suffer when inflation rates unexpectedly rise.

So those who would have us consider the purchasing power gains on corporate debt have a point. However, when inflation is expected by borrowers and lenders alike, debt yields tend to include an inflation premium to compensate creditors for the lost purchasing power on their loans. When inflation rates rose unexpectedly during the 1970s, the purchasing power holding gains on outstanding corporate debt were not immediately offset by larger inflation premiums in debt service charges. Those who have added these holding gains to corporate profits have often wondered why stock prices are so low.[3] Despite these high adjusted "profits," stock prices are low because current profits do not yet reflect the eventual increase in financing costs. Investors must appraise *prospective* profits to value equity. Stockholders should expect no significant, lasting benefit at the expense of bondholders: because the full inflation premium is not

---

[3] For example, Modigliani and Cohn, Chapter 6.

56

yet embodied in current debt service charges, the full advantage of purchasing power holding gains on debt is only temporary, and these gains, while they last, are roughly offset by matching purchasing power losses on pension fund reserves.

Conclusion

Inflation can influence stock prices in many ways. I have limited my discussion to the influences that I believe are most important. Even the analysis of taxes and holding gains on debt is far more complicated than the highlights I have sketched here. Nevertheless, no matter how extensive or how complicated the analysis might become, the conclusion remains that stocks have been and will remain a poor hedge against unexpected changes in the inflation rate. In other words, the sour performance of major equity indexes in the past 10 years was no fluke. If inflation unexpectedly soars during the next 10 years, investors can expect more real losses. Conversely, if the rate of inflation should drop to an unexpectedly low level or if business income taxes are indexed, the age of customer yachts and fat foundations may return, fund managers may once again become sought-after gurus, and brokers may once again sport the Gucci label.

Stocks are not now a bargain, nor are they dear—they are just risky. Should the inflation rate not change in coming years, investors will earn lucrative returns for bearing that risk. Should the inflation rate unexpectedly rise, investors will know why they were paid for taking that risk.

4

The Myth of Common Stocks and Inflation

by

Steven C. Leuthold

THE MYTH OF COMMON STOCKS AND INFLATION

by Steven C. Leuthold

In the halcyon days of the 1960s, when the stock market seemed to be marching forever onward and upward, almost all investors believed the stock market was a hedge against inflation. Indeed, it was commonly believed that inflation was good for the stock market.

Then, as inflation surged ahead in the 1970s and the stock market surged down, investors began to question the prevailing wisdom about the stock market and inflation. Perhaps, they thought, the stock market was not a hedge against inflation. Perhaps inflation was bad for the stock market. Currently there is a growing belief that deflation would be good for the stock market. We also have some frustrated investors who say nothing is good for the stock market.

Strangely, those frustrated investors may be closest to the truth, because our research demonstrates that the best stock market performance takes place in years of price stability— years when essentially nothing is happening on the inflation/ deflation front; years when the cost of goods and services is up or down 1 percent or less. Thus, at least in terms of inflation and deflation, nothing is good for the stock market.

Many investors will say this is not a particularly stunning revelation, but other aspects of our research, some highlighted herein, will provide new insights into the stock market's relationship with and response to various levels of inflation and deflation.

When the early stages of this work were presented by the Leuthold Group in 1975, its conclusions surprised most pro-

---

This chapter draws on the research reported in my recent book, *The Myths of Inflation and Investing* (Chicago: Crain Books, 1980).

fessional investors because apparently no one had bothered to research the validity of the idea of stocks as an inflation hedge. Wall Street and the investment business in general, even in this age of computerization and informational sophistication, often seems mired in myths, folklore, clichés, old wives' tales, and tradition.

History as a guide

So let's look at the facts. Let us take a good look at the past relationship between inflationary years and the stock market movements, and between deflationary years and the stock market movements. History, while not always providing definitive answers, can be a most helpful guide.

For this purpose we dug out the level of annual inflation or deflation in the U.S. economy during the past 108 years, 1872 through 1979, using the consumer price index or a predecessor as proxy. Then we calculated the annual percentage changes of the stock market, excluding dividends. For the 1872-1936 period we used the Cowles All Stocks Index as a source. From that point on, we used the Dow Jones Industrial Average. The DJIA was used for this later period because it was convenient and widely followed, not because it was the best index.

Finally, we divided the 108 years of economic and market history into six environments:

1. *Years of extraordinary inflation.* In these years inflation ranged from 8 percent to 18 percent. We found that 13 percent of the years studied (14 of the 108) fell into this category.
2. *Years of relatively high inflation.* These ranged from 4 percent to 7 percent inflation per year. Some 18.5 percent of the years studied (20 of 108 years) fell into this category.
3. *Years of moderate inflation.* Inflation ranged from 2 per-

cent to 3 percent per year, and 19.4 percent of the years (21 of 108) fell into this category.

4. *Years of price stability.* The range was from 1 percent inflation to 1 percent deflation, and 27.8 percent of the years (30 of 108) met this qualification.

5. *Years of moderate deflation.* Annual deflation rates ranged from 2 percent to 4 percent, and 12 percent of the years studied (13 of 108) fell into this category.

6. *Years of extraordinary deflation.* The annual deflation rate ranged from 5 percent to 11 percent. Only 9.3 percent of the years (10 of 108) fell into this category.

Thus there were 55 years of inflation (extraordinary, relatively high, or moderate), 23 years of deflation (moderate or extraordinary), and 30 years of relative price stability. Inflation, therefore, has not been a constant factor with which investors have had to contend. But what has its impact been on stock market investments, investments which many people felt provided the best protection against inflation's ravages?

The tables and charts herein provide part of the answer. They assume that a theoretical investor owned stocks only in the years which qualified for a particular category of inflation or deflation years. In reality, of course, these qualifying years were not consecutive. But the calculation is still an effective way to demonstrate the relative investment attractiveness of each environment.

How has the market performed during the whole 108-year period? It was up in 61.1 percent, or 66, of the years, with a median gain of 15.1 percent in the rising years. It was down in 38.9 percent of the years, with a median loss of 12.3 percent. The median-year performance was a gain of 3.3 percent, and the compound annual return for the whole period was 2.6 percent. These figures do not include dividends. Dividends averaged about 4.8 percent, indicating a compound annual total return rate of about 7.4 percent from 1872 through the end of 1978. But this is only part of the picture.

63

A clearer picture emerges if we look separately at each category.

A deeper look

If an investor put money into the market only during the years of extraordinary inflation (when it ranged between 8 percent and 18 percent), he would have been invested for 14 years. Assuming that the starting value was $1,000 and that those years were consecutive, the terminal value of the initial investment would be only $821, for a compound annual loss of 1.4 percent. Years of extraordinary inflation thus appear to be poor years for stock market investments.

Years of relatively high inflation are even worse. The investor could have been in the market for 20 such years in the period under examination, and his $1,000 investment would have declined to $296, for a compound annual loss of 5.9 percent.

Years of moderate inflation provide better results. There were 21 such years in our survey period, and a $1,000 investment would have grown in an environment of 2-3 percent inflation to $4,223, for a compound annual return of 7.1 percent.

There were 30 years of relative stability in our survey period, and a $1,000 investment in these years would have produced a terminal value of $10,063, or a compound annual growth rate of 8 percent.

Years of moderate deflation would have produced a compound annual growth rate of 7.8 percent, giving a terminal value of $2,655 after 13 years.

Finally, years of extraordinary deflation, of which there were 10 in the period examined, were as bad for the stock market as years of relatively high inflation, reducing the starting value of $1,000 to only $544, for a compound annual decline of 5.9 percent.

These results are summarized in Table 4-1 and Figure 4-1.

Table 4-1: Theoretical investment results (starting capital: $1,000)

Environment	Years invested	Starting value	Terminal value	Compound annual growth
Extraordinary inflation (8%-18%) 14		$1,000	$ 821	−1.4%
Relatively high inflation (4%-7%) 20		1,000	296	−5.9
Moderate inflation (2%-3%) 21		1,000	4,223	7.1
Stability (1% inflation-1% deflation) 30		1,000	10,063	8.0
Moderate deflation (2%-4%) 13		1,000	2,655	7.8
Extraordinary deflation (5%-11%) 10		1,000	544	−5.9

Figure 4-1: 108 years of investing (1872-1979) in six inflationary/deflationary environments (annual compound rate)

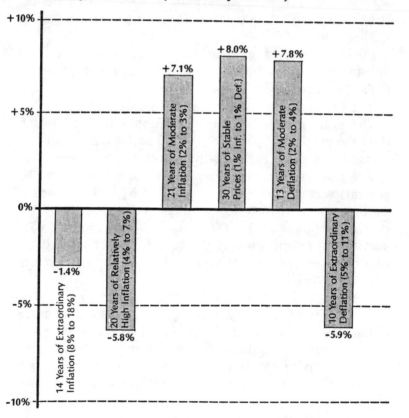

65

The question arises as to why the extraordinary inflation was less damaging to a $1,000 investment than the relatively high inflation. In part, this may be the result of a statistical quirk. But it also reflects the fact that in some of the years of extraordinary inflation the inflation rate was decelerating, and, as will be discussed later, a decelerating rate of inflation is good for the stock market.

Adjusting the picture

But these figures give only half of the picture because they do not take into consideration the annual loss or gain in buying power caused by the annual rate of inflation or deflation. If we adjust the return picture to constant dollars, it changes significantly.

First, the years of extraordinary inflation were the worst investment environment because the purchasing power of $1,000 declined to only $138 during the 14 years, giving a compound annual negative return of 13.2 percent.

The years of relatively high inflation were little better. Here the purchasing power of $1,000 declined during the 20 years to only $166, for a negative return of 8.6 percent.

The real return during periods of moderate inflation (2-3 percent) was 4.6 percent, as the initial $1,000 increased in buying power to $2,571. In the 30 years of stability the purchasing power of $1,000 increased to $9,257, for a 7.7 percent real return, while in the 13 years of moderate deflation (2-4 percent) it increased to $3,577, for a real return of 10.3 percent.

Even extraordinary deflation provided a better return than extraordinary or relatively high inflation. In periods of extraordinary deflation, although the initial $1,000 declined to $544 in the market, its purchasing power actually increased to $1,027, giving a constant dollar compound annual growth rate of 1.9 percent. These results are shown in Table 4-2 and Figure 4-2.

In terms of real purchasing power, therefore, periods of

66

Table 4-2: Constant dollar compound annual growth

Environment	Years invested	Starting value	Constant dollar terminal value	Constant dollar compound annual growth
Extraordinary inflation (8%-18%) 14		$1,000	$ 138	−13.2%
Relatively high inflation (4%-7%) 20		1,000	166	− 8.6
Moderate inflation (2%-3%) 21		1,000	2,571	4.6
Stability (1% inflation-1% deflation)... 30		1,000	9,257	7.7
Moderate deflation (2%-4%) 13		1,000	3,577	10.3
Extraordinary deflation (5%-11%) 10		1,000	1,207	1.9

moderate deflation have been the best for the stock market investor. While the market has not increased as much in these periods as in periods of relative stability, with the decline in prices it has increased sufficiently to make the constant dollar return greatest.

Unfortunately for the stock market investor, years of moderate deflation are not as common as years of moderate inflation or of relatively high inflation, and years of extraordinary inflation, the worst of all possible environments, are just as common as years of moderate deflation.

Happily, the second best environment in terms of constant dollar returns, years of relative price stability, has also been the most common environment. In the years when the inflation rate or the deflation rate was 1 percent or less, the constant dollar compound annual rate of growth was 7.7 percent. As we noted above, the 30 years of relative price stability provided the best environment purely in terms of market returns.

Decelerating and accelerating inflation

When economic history and stock market performance are rubbed together, the evidence is overwhelming that the stock market performs below average during periods of more than 4 percent inflation, while in periods of relative price stability

67

Figure 4-2: 108 years of investing (1872-1979) in six inflationary/
deflationary environments (constant dollars, adjusted for
inflation/deflation)

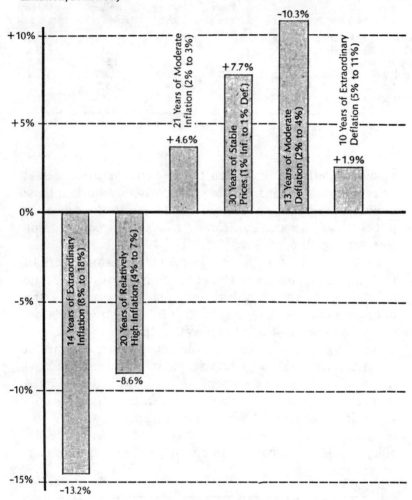

or perhaps even mild inflation, its performance is significantly above average.

But what happens to the stock market when inflation is accelerating or decelerating?

To provide some insights into this question, we isolated all the years from 1900 to 1979 in which inflation was 4 percent and above and in which inflation had accelerated at least 2 percent from the prior year. We also tracked the stock market performance for these years. Table 4-3 presents the results of the 17 years when inflation was accelerating. The Cowles Commission Index and the Dow Jones Industrial Average were once again used as the stock market proxy.

Tables 4-3 and 4-4 show several interesting things. First, even though the actual up years and down years are almost balanced (eight up, nine down), the losing years were really big losers, declining an average 20 percent. Also, the years of market advance were marginal at best, averaging 5 percent. The biggest nominal winner was 1951, which had a 14.4 percent gain.

Table 4-3: 17 inflation acceleration years, 1900-1979

Year	Inflation level	Preceding year's inflation	Percent increase	Stock market	Net change in constant dollar (inflation adjusted)
1902	4%	2%	2%	1.3%	− 2.7%
1906	4	−	4	3.2	− 0.8
1910	4	−	4	−12.3	−16.3
1912	4	−	4	2.9	− 1.1
1916	8	1	7	3.4	− 4.6
1917	17	8	9	−30.7	−47.7
1937	4	−	4	−32.8	−36.8
1941	5	1	4	−15.4	−20.4
1942	11	5	6	7.6	− 3.4
1946	9	2	7	− 8.1	−17.1
1947	14	9	5	2.2	−11.8
1951	8	1	7	14.4	6.4
1957	4	2	2	−12.8	−16.8
1973	6	3	3	−16.6	−22.6
1974	11	6	5	−27.6	−38.6
1978	9	7	2	− 3.2	−12.2
1979	13	9	4	4.2	− 8.8

Table 4-4: Summary of 17 inflation acceleration years,
1900-1979

	Nominal dollars	Constant dollars
Up years	8	1
Down years	9	16
All 17 years		
Median annual performance	−3.2%	−12.2%
Average annual performance	−7.1%	−15.0%
Hypothetical annual compound loss		
(17 years linked)	−8.2%	−16.4%

When viewed in terms of constant dollars, taking into consideration the dollar erosion from each year's inflation rate, 1951 was the single winning year in the 17 years examined, and the gain was only 6.4 percent. Overall, relative investment performance for these inflation acceleration years is miserable, whether measured in nominal or constant dollars.

The largest nominal loss in inflation acceleration years was 32.8 percent in 1937, when inflation increased from zero the previous year to 4 percent. The second biggest nominal loss was 30.7 percent in 1917, when the inflation rate more than doubled, from 8 percent in 1916 to 17 percent in 1917. More recently, when inflation almost doubled, from 6 percent in 1973 to 11 percent in 1974, the market lost 27.6 percent.

Rapidly accelerating inflation, particularly if it is from a level of 4 percent or more, is a hostile environment for the stock market investor. If the investor can strongly support a conclusion that a current inflation level of 4 percent or higher will increase by 2 percent or more in the next 12 months, he should realize he probably has two strikes against him.

Essentially the same procedure has been followed in examining years from 1900 to date when inflation was decelerating. Inflation deceleration years are identified as years in which inflation declined at least 2 percent from a preceding significant inflation year (4 percent and above). Sixteen years fit this definition. Note that some high-inflation years, such as 1919 (15 percent) and 1975 (9 percent), also qualify as inflation deceleration years because inflation, though still high, was coming down.

We find that 16 years fitted our selected criteria, and 14 of these years recorded gains in nominal dollars, ranging from 38 percent in 1975 and 37 percent in 1908 to 6 percent in 1971 (see Tables 4-5 and 4-6). Only 1913 (−14 percent) was a significant losing year. More important perhaps, in constant dollars there were only 3 losing years out of the 16. All in all, these look like pretty good odds.

Thus periods of decelerating inflation appear to be very positive investment environments. And even though the actual level of inflation may still be high by historic standards, the more important factor is the *declining* trend. Investor recognition of inflation deceleration from levels of 4 percent and above would appear to be a significant factor, improving the odds of investment success.

Table 4-5: Inflation deceleration years 1900-1979

Year	Inflation level	Preceding year's inflation	Percent decrease	Stock market	Net change in constant dollar (inflation adjusted)
1900	2%	7%	5%	14.1%	12.1%
1904	0	4	4	25.6	25.6
1908 . . . . . . −	3	4	7	37.3	40.3
1911	0	4	4	1.0	1.0
1913 . . . . . . −	1	4	5	−14.2	−13.2
1919	15	18	3	13.1	− 1.9
1921	−11	16	27	7.3	18.3
1938 . . . . . . −	2	4	6	28.1	30.1
1943	6	11	5	13.8	7.8
1944	2	6	4	12.1	10.1
1948	8	14	6	− 2.1	−10.1
1949 . . . . . . −	1	8	7	12.9	13.9
1952	2	8	6	8.4	6.4
1971	4	6	2	6.1	2.1
1975	9	11	2	38.3	29.3
1976	6	9	3	17.6	11.6

71

Table 4-6: Summary of 16 inflation deceleration years, 1900-1979

	Nominal dollars	Constant dollars
Up years	14	13
Down years	2	3
All 16 years		
Median annual performance	13.0%	10.9%
Average annual performance	13.7%	11.5%
Hypothetical annual compound gain (16 years linked)	12.9%	10.6%

Inflation and price-earnings multiples

As has been demonstrated earlier, the stock market typically performs below average when inflation is 4 percent or more, and when prices are relatively stable, stock market performance is significantly above average.

To reinforce the view that inflation is viewed properly as a negative stock market influence (except when inflation is decelerating), an examination should be made of consumer price index (CPI) trends and historic common stock valuations, using annual prevailing normalized price-earnings multiples as the valuation standard. What follows may provide some useful and definitive benchmarks for investors to apply in various inflation environments.

P/E multiples as benchmarks

The most widely used tool in security analysis is the price-earnings ratio. This ratio allows the investor to compare the relative values of individual stocks with their earnings. Although the P/E multiple is typically used in comparing individual issues, it can also be used for the stock market as a whole.

The P/E ratio is often a good benchmark to gauge valua-

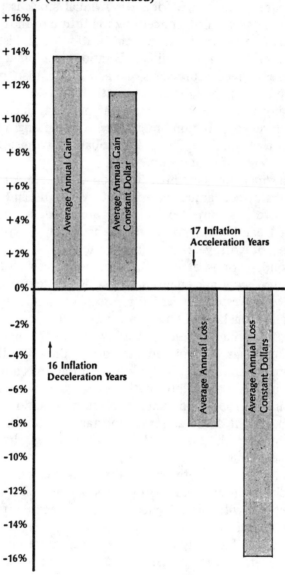

Figure 4-3: Comparative stock market investment results for periods studied, 1900-1979 (dividends excluded)

73

tions—and investor psychology. In its simplest application, the higher the P/E, the more optimistic investors are about the future. A high P/E for an individual stock is usually a reflection of optimism concerning the future of the economy. Obviously, this is an oversimplification, but history has demonstrated that prevailing P/E ratios are more a function of current greed, apprehension, and panic than of future realized earnings and dividend growth.

At any rate, the historical research clearly indicates that higher levels of inflation bring lower price-earnings valuations in the stock market. There are probably two major reasons why this kind of relationship exists.

First, in periods of high inflation corporate earnings are often distorted, larded with inventory profits and the like. Many investors may view this inflation-produced portion of reported earnings as nonrecurring, artificial, or "poor quality," or not worthy of a typical P/E multiple.

Second, periods of high inflation reflect an unstable and vulnerable economic environment, which fosters an abnormal degree of investor concern for future economic health and results in a lack of enthusiasm for common stock investing. Lack of confidence results in a lower value being placed on future earnings. As pointed out earlier, the myth that common stocks are a good hedge against inflation is not substantiated historically. Although this credo gained broad acceptance in the 1950s and 1960s, it is far more fiction than fact.

Some might argue a third important reason for this relationship, something along the following lines: Higher inflation means higher interest rates. Higher interest rates mean tougher bond competition for the stock market on a total risk-adjusted return basis. So if the stock market is to remain competitive with these higher bond interest rates, it must sell below its typical valuation.

While this factor appears to have been quite important in recent years, the longer term documentation is less decisive. For example, our 200-year analysis of inflation and interest rates raises some doubts that higher inflation means higher interest rates. Well . . . it ain't necessarily so.

Comment on techniques

Comparing P/E multiples based on most recent 12-month earnings is of limited analytical value, especially when the earnings are cyclical in nature. Cyclical earnings must be normalized, smoothed out, or averaged, typically over three to five years, before meaningful relative comparisons can be made. Analysis of the raw cyclical data can result in erroneous conclusions.

In this study we used a three-year centered average of the earnings (last year, this year, next year) for the market as a whole, using 108 years of data (1872 to 1979). This yielded 107 years of annual data without making a 1980 earnings projection. Again, the Cowles Commission Index was used for the early years, and the Dow Jones Industrial Average for the more recent years. The years 1931 through 1934 were excluded from some of the statistical presentations because of their distortion effect.

It should also be noted that the annual P/E data presented are based on the average market index price that prevailed in each year. Extreme intrayear highs and lows are not isolated. They are averaged right in with all the other days. Readers should keep in mind that the extremes noted in this study are not the absolute zeniths and nadirs of market peaks and market bottoms.

Let's see what happens to P/E ratios in various inflation/ deflation environments. Table 4-7 shows us.

As can be seen from Table 4-7 and from the aggregate table (Table 4-8), following P/E ratios decline steadily once inflation exceeds 4 percent. Between 6 percent deflation and 4 percent inflation, the P/E ratio moves between 14 times and almost 16 times earnings (15.8 times, to be precise). At 5 percent to 6 percent inflation, it begins to decline steadily,

Table 4-7

Inflation/deflation	Years included	Average P/E	Median P/E
Deflation 6% or more	7	14.7	12.9
Deflation 3% to 5%	6	15.2	14.9
Deflation 2%	10	13.7	13.3
Deflation 1%	5	13.8	14.1
0	11	15.8	13.9
Inflation 1%.	14	13.9	13.5
Inflation 2%.	14	15.1	14.9
Inflation 3%.	7	14.6	15.3
Inflation 4%.	10	14.6	14.6
Inflation 5% to 6%	7	13.2	11.7
Inflation 7% to 8%	6	10.7	9.3
Inflation 9% to 11%	5	9.9	9.0
Inflation 12% or more	5	8.9	9.6

Table 4-8

	Average P/E	Median P/E
80 years, inflation less than 5%	15.2	14.6
7 years, inflation 5% to 6%.	13.2	11.7
6 years, inflation 7% to 8%.	10.7	9.3
5 years, inflation 9% to 11%	9.9	9.0
5 years, inflation 12% plus	8.9	9.6
103 years (excludes 1931-34)	14.6	14.1

falling below nine times earnings when inflation reaches 12 percent or more.

The study shows that the median P/E ratio was 14.1 times earnings during the 1872-1978 period (excluding 1931 through 1934), while the average P/E for the period was 14.6. Bear in mind that the median annual inflation rate for the period was 1.5 percent and the annual compound rate was 1.8 percent. Also remember that there were 68 years of inflation (1 percent or more), 28 years of deflation (1 percent or more), and only 11 years of no change.

When the years of 5 percent inflation or more are excluded, the median historic P/E for the market advances 3.5 percent, from 14.1 to 14.6, and the average historic P/E advances 4 percent, from 14.6 to 15.2 (see Figure 4-4 and Table 4-8).

The highest average P/E ratio occurred in periods of zero inflation. During the 11 years of zero inflation, the market P/E averaged 15.8, though the median was lower, at 13.9. The next highest average P/E occurred during periods of 3 percent to 5 percent deflation. During the six years that met this criterion, the average P/E was 15.2 and the median was

Figure 4-4: Impact of inflation on P/E multiples, 1872-1978 (1931-1934 omitted)

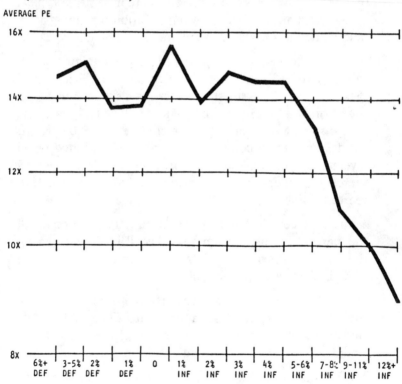

Average annual P/E (three-year-earnings centered) for the market, using Cowles Composite Index and The Dow Jones Industrials as bases.

14.9. The sample is small, so don't assign much significance to this statistic.

Inflation earnings valuation benchmarks

The data suggest the following valuation guidelines. Average data and median data were considered in arriving at these discount benchmarks. Average data are arrived at by adding up the individual years and dividing by the number in the sample. The median is the point where half the numbers in the sample are above and half below. Use of the median minimizes distortion years.

14.5 to 15 times normalized earnings represent the typical market valuation of stocks when inflation is running at an annual rate less than 5 percent and deflation exists.

When inflation is in the 5 percent to 6 percent zone, a P/E discount of 15 percent seems appropriate. Since only 7 years of the 108 years studied are in this zone, one might question the validity of this benchmark. At any rate, the P/E discount calculated using median data is 20 percent. And a smaller discount of 13 percent is indicated when average P/E data are used. Our rule of thumb will be a 15 percent discount in this environment of 5 percent to 6 percent inflation.

In the 7 percent to 8 percent inflation range, a discount of 33 percent seems appropriate. (The P/E discount calculated using the median data is 36 percent; the average data indicate a 30 percent discount.)

In the 9 percent to 11 percent inflation range, a P/E discount of 36 percent seems appropriate. (The median data indicate a P/E discount of 36 percent; the average data indicate a 34 percent discount.)

When inflation blazes at 12 percent and above, a 38 percent P/E discount seems appropriate. A caveat: This discount is based on only five years of experience at these runaway inflation levels, although 1979's 13 percent inflation and 1980's 12 percent inflation give us seven years. The range in discounts runs from 55 percent in 1917 to 20 percent in 1920. If 1979's and 1980's discounts are factored in, this typical discount rises, but only to about 39 percent.

One thing is quite clear. A significant decline in the rate of inflation in coming years would imply a mouth-watering degree of upside potential for the stock market—almost 100 percent above current levels if inflation backed down to 5 percent. And that is assuming *no* earnings growth.

In conclusion

Although the research indicating that a correlation exists between annual stock market movements and the annual rate of inflation or deflation is helpful to the investor, this information does not qualify as an investment panacea. It is not a magic key to successful investment strategy because it depends on one's ability to predict inflation or deflation levels a year in advance. And predicting next year's inflation or deflation, especially when inflation is currently high, could be as difficult as predicting next year's stock market.

Contrary to what might be expected, the shift from an inflationary to a deflationary environment need not be gradual. It can be quite abrupt. For example, the country suffered through 15 percent inflation in 1919 and through 16 percent inflation in 1920, but in 1921 it had 11 percent deflation. Similarly, 14 percent inflation in 1947 was followed by 8 percent inflation in 1948 and then by 1 percent deflation in 1949.

What, then, of those who say the stock market is a long-term hedge against inflation? The believers usually cited long-term stock market investment results for, say, 25 years, 50 years, or more, and comparing these with the long-term inflation rate. Because the stock market gained more than was lost to inflation during this period, the believers conclude that stocks are a hedge against inflation.

This is, at best, a questionable conclusion. In all of the time periods we studied, stock market growth rates most closely correlated with book value growth, earnings growth, and dividends growth. The stock market gains during these periods were recognition of these fundamental growth factors. These are the prime movers, not inflation. If the long-term growth of these fundamental factors slows down or ceases, the stock market will follow suit even if inflation continues to surge ahead.

5

U.S. Equities as an Inflation Hedge

by

Burton G. Malkiel

U.S. EQUITIES AS AN INFLATION HEDGE
by Burton G. Malkiel

Back in the olden days, defined by my nine-year-old son as the years before he was born, it was widely believed that sensible investors should buy common stocks for generous long-run returns and for protection against inflation. Over the long pull, common stocks had produced an annual rate of return of more than 9 percent—considerably above the long-run rate of inflation. And since equities represent ownership claims on real property, in principle they should provide investors with long-run protection against inflation. After all, in an era of inflation, factories, equipment, and inventories should rise in value along with all other prices.

Yet today, even after a strong market through most of 1980, there is serious question whether common stocks are, in fact, an inflation hedge. The experience of the 1970s certainly created many doubters among professional as well as nonprofessional investors. The DJIA which supposedly had crossed the 1,000 mark for good ended the decade of the 1970s still languishing near the 800 level. True, the Dow was a particularly bad performer. Nevertheless, between 1968 and 1979 the annual rate of return on broader indexes of U.S. common stocks (including dividends as well as capital changes) was a paltry 3.1 percent. The annual rate of return for gold and various objets d'art was more than six times that of stocks.

Because this disastrous performance occurred at the same time the general price level doubled, it became fashionable to believe that stocks were no longer an effective hedge against inflation (if they ever were). Indeed, astute financial writers, such as Warren Buffett, claim that inflation destroys real earnings power and "swindles the equity investor."[1] In 1979 *Business Week* published a cover story on the death of equities. Academics began producing statistical studies showing a negative correlation between changes in the level of stock prices and changes in the rate of inflation. Institutional investors who did not believe in capital punishment understandably rushed to the sidelines, and individuals were consistent net sellers of their equity mutual funds. As I put it in a book which went to press in January 1980, "As the decade of the 1980s began, few people were thanking Paine Webber, and even when E. F. Hutton talked, nobody listened."[2]

It reminded one of the small boy who on his first trip to an art museum was told that a famous abstract painting was supposed to be a horse. "Well, then," the boy demanded, "if it's supposed to be a horse, why isn't it?" If common stocks are supposed to be an inflation hedge, why weren't they in the 1970s?

The dissatisfaction with equities goes deeper, however, than impatience with their performance during any particular period or their negative short-run correlation with inflation. Many institutional investors still wonder whether common stocks can, over the long run, protect against inflation. These Wall Street naysayers proclaim that inflation has caused corporate profits and dividend-paying ability to shrink drastically, especially when appropriate inflation adjustments are made to the reported figures. Inflation is often portrayed as a kind of financial neutron bomb, leaving the structure of corporate enterprise intact but destroying the lifeblood of profits. In effect, this is a belief in a fundamental change in our economic system, a change in which profits will never return to former levels, but rather will continue to decline without interruption. Since profits are the source of dividends and since increased earnings provide the underpinning for capital gains, these doomsayers see nothing but trouble

---

[1] See Chapter 2.

[2] *The Inflation Beaters Investment Guide* (New York: W. W. Norton, 1980).

for the stock market. Writers such as Basil Moore believe that they have already detected some shrinkage of real (inflation-adjusted) dividends.[3] Consequently, some observers see the engine of capitalism running in reverse, and in such a case a walk down Wall Street—random or otherwise—is quite unhealthy.

The specific thesis of those who take a more or less apocalyptic view of the world is that aftertax profits as a percentage of invested capital have shrunk considerably, especially over the late 1960s and early 1970s. But is the world such a depressing place these days? Have corporate profits become an illusion? Let's round up the suspects, chief among them the alleged profits squeeze, and see who or what caused the market's sorry performance in the 1970s. Let's first recognize that figuring out true profitability during a period of inflation is quite complex. Profits are swelled during inflationary periods by two fictitious elements: (1) the inclusion of inventory profits and (2) the calculation of depreciation allowances on an original cost basis rather than a replacement cost basis.

Inventory profits are not the benefit to a firm that they seem. As the firm disposes of its appreciated inventory, the goods must be replaced at higher prices. Thus inventory profits provide no cash flow for the firm. Indeed, just the opposite is true, for unlike unrealized gains on plant, these paper profits are taxed at regular income tax rates.

Depreciation charges are another factor in the inflation-swollen profit picture. Because depreciation charges are based on low original rather than higher current replacement cost, they are usually not as high as they should be. This makes the remaining income appear as healthy profit when it should be set aside to provide for the necessary replacement of the depreciating assets. It also makes taxes higher than they should be. So in looking at profit numbers, it is important not to take them as reported but to exclude inventory

---

[3] See Chapter 7.

profits and raise depreciation charges to the economically relevant replacement cost basis.

Most people forget there is a further necessary inflation adjustment to reported profits: inflation reduces the real value of the firm's debt. Current accounting conventions ignore this fact. It is well known that bondholders suffer from inflation because they get paid back in dollars that have less purchasing power than the dollars originally invested. But the counterpart of the bond investors' loss is the bond issuers' gain. This gain never shows up in any of our profit figures— even the ones supposedly adjusted to account for inflation. For example, suppose Dow Chemical sold a 30-year, 4 percent bond in 1951. Clearly the bondholder has lost out. The bondholder will get paid back in 1981 in dollars with far less purchasing power (even including accumulated interest) than was originally invested. But who gained? Obviously Dow Chemical and its shareholders gained.

OK, you say, but that bond was issued when inflation was unanticipated. We didn't think inflation was a fact of life in 1950. That is why interest rates were so low. In 1980, Dow might have had to pay 12 to 13 percent for long-term money; so an investor could obtain a 3 percent real rate of return and inflation protection of 9 or 10 percent. Thus today there are 9 to 10 points of inflation premiums in interest rates to compensate for the confiscation of purchasing power from the bondholder. But this is just the point. Our accounting conventions deduct all interest (including the inflation premium) from operating income, but we never include the transfer from the bondholder to the stockholder that comes from decline in the real value of the debt and is the cause of the inflation premium.

Figure 5-1 presents the development of fully adjusted aftertax corporate profits in the United States over the past quarter-century. Reported profits are adjusted to exclude inventory profits, to put depreciation on a replacement cost basis, and to add back to profits the decline in the real value

Figure 5-1: Inflation-adjusted profits related to replacement value of equity capital

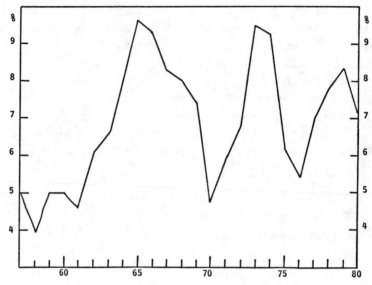

Source: Council of Economic Advisers.

of corporate debt. These adjusted profits are related to the value of stockholders' equity at *replacement cost.* The numbers show no evidence that corporate profitability is in a long-run decline. While profits in the mid-1970s were certainly lower than they were in the mid-1960s, they were considerably higher in the late 1970s than they were in the late 1950s and early 1960s.

Of course, the adjusted profit numbers declined in 1980, just as they did in the 1974-75 recession. But profits do not appear to have fallen nearly as sharply as they did in that recession, and there is simply no evidence that over the long pull true profits have been "sliding down a pole greased by cruel and inexorable inflation," as is widely believed in the financial community. On this point I agree completely with

Modigliani and Cohn, who also argue that true profits are much healthier than is commonly supposed.[4] Moreover, unlike Kopcke, I do not find that the effective tax rate on true business income has risen, at least at the corporate level, when all aspects of inflationary adjustments are taken into account, including the untaxed gains from the reduction of real indebtedness.[5]

Perhaps, however, we are looking in the wrong place for a clue to the market's decline. Remember the well-known story of the government bureaucrat searching on his hands and knees on Pennsylvania Avenue during the midday rush:

"What are you looking for?" asked a passerby.

"My watch."

"Do you remember where you lost it?"

"Over on Connecticut Avenue."

"Then why are you looking here?"

"The light is better here."

Much light is placed on corporate earnings in the financial press, but perhaps the experts would be wiser to focus on dividends rather than earnings. Maybe the relevant question is not what earnings show—however adjusted—but rather what dividends U.S. corporations are able to pay. The acid test of whether true earning power is increasing is the ability of corporations to provide a stream of dividends whose growth will keep up with inflation. Let us, then, move our light from earnings to dividends.

Figure 5-2 shows the progression of dividends over the 1960s and 1970s as well as the inexorable upward march of the price level as measured by the consumer price index. It shows clearly that dividends from the major U.S. corporations (as measured by the Standard & Poor's Composite Index) have outpaced inflation. Even more exciting is an index

---

[4] See Chapter 6.
[5] See Chapter 3.

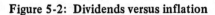

Figure 5-2: Dividends versus inflation

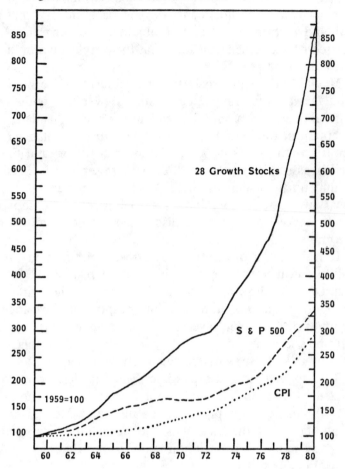

of the dividends of 28 growth companies compiled by David L. Babson & Co.; it far outdistanced the CPI. Dividend growth greater than inflation doesn't happen in every year. It didn't happen in 1974-75, and it didn't happen in 1980. Moreover, as Basil Moore has pointed out, you can pick a base date during the 1960s from which dividend growth did not quite keep up with the CPI. But the long-run picture is

89

still intact—dividends have outpaced inflation. If you don't like my earnings adjustment, I come back and say that the dividend picture is just as favorable over the long pull. I do not see how one can conclude that the problem lies in inadequate dividend growth.

Movie buffs will recall the marvelous final scene from *Casablanca.* Humphrey Bogart stands over the body of a Luftwaffe major, a smoking gun in his hand. Claude Rains, a captain in the French Colonial Police, turns his glance from Bogart to the smoking gun, to the dead major, and finally to his assistant, and says, "Major Strasser has been shot. Round up the usual suspects." We too have rounded up the usual suspects, but we have yet to find out who shot the stock market, nor have we discovered a rational motive for the crime.

If it is not a precipitate and irreversible drop in profitability and dividend-paying ability that is responsible for the market's bad showing in the 1970s, why did the market do so poorly? The major reason for the poor performance of equity prices is that investors' evaluation of earnings—the multiples they are willing to pay for a dollar of earnings—fell roughly in half. But why did the multiples collapse?

Two explanations are possible. The first has been popularized by Franco Modigliani and Richard Cohn, who argue that the maket is simply making a mistake.[6] Modigliani and Cohn state that the market is just not capitalizing earnings properly in an era of inflation and that multiples have fallen to irrationally low levels.

This explanation is, of course, quite plausible. Markets often overreact and get carried away in frenzies of speculative buying and fits of selling panic. The market may now be irrationally pessimistic, as perhaps it was unreasonably optimistic in the 1960s. Nevertheless, I do not find this explanation entirely convincing. While I am not a dyed-in-the-wool

---

[6] Franco Modigliani and Richard Cohn present their argument in Chapter 6, together with new evidence from their recent researches.

efficient marketeer, and while I don't argue that market prices are always correct, I do have a healthy respect for the market's judgment. Between the economics profession and the stock market, I would still place my bet on the stock market every time.

In my judgment the problem may not be that the market is stupid—but rather that it is scared. Investors may not be making a mistake, but rather thay may now *correctly* demand much higher prospective rates of return from common stocks to compensate them for the sharply increased risk perceptions they see. In other words, investors now demand higher risk premiums. Investors in the mid- to late-1960s saw the economic environment as a very stable one and faced the future with feelings of consummate confidence. From the middle of the 1970s to the end of the decade, investors had good reason to view the economy as far less stable and they looked to the future with considerable uncertainty.

In the mid-1960s inflation was only beginning to rear its ugly head and consumer prices had been relatively stable for a number of years. We even thought in those days we could manipulate the economy so that recessions could be "fine-tuned" away; and we considered depressions a curious anachronism. In short, the world seemed very stable. In retrospect, it is clear that this confidence and the associated high multiples assigned to earnings were not justified. Today, in contrast, there is in our country an almost palpable mood of uncertainty and pessimism. Who would have believed 10 years ago that we could go through a period when the unemployment rate would approach 9 percent or the inflation rate would be measured in double digits, let alone when both would occur simultaneously, as they did in the mid-1970s? Despite the 1980 recession the inflation rate remained at unprecedentedly high levels more usually associated with a banana republic than with the U.S. economy. This instability in our economic system has generated a mood of anxiety and foreboding about the future of the economy and about our ability to cope with our current economic problems.

91

Thus corporations' earnings available for their equity securities (dare I say equity insecurities?) became quite rationally considered more variable and less dependable. Indeed, as investor sentiment shifted to a fuller recognition of the risks of equity ownership, there may well have been an excessive reaction. There was a tendency for uncertainty to turn to extreme pessimism. Murphy's law, "What can go wrong will go wrong," was replaced by O'Toole's commentary, "Murphy was an optimist." As a consequence, investors became reluctant to hold equities unless the prospective returns were raised by an increased "risk premium" appropriate to the new higher level of risk associated with equity ownership. Ironically, this was accomplished through a decline in stock prices relative to earnings so as to provide larger future returns consistent with the new, riskier environment. Precisely because equities were perceived as riskier, investors marked down equity prices so that stocks could provide in the future an appropriately higher expected rate of return as compared with less risky assets.[7]

In my view the behavior of the stock market in the 1970s was strongly affected by a very sharp increase in the risk perceptions of investors. This, in turn, caused a devastating markdown in price-earnings multiples. In early 1973 investors paid over $18 for a dollar of earnings for the Standard & Poor's Composite Index. By early 1980 a dollar of the same earnings commanded only about $8 in the market. (See Figure 5-3.) Multiples of fast-growing companies suffered an even sharper drop. In early 1973 the multiple for the David Babson index of growth stocks (whose dividend growth was

---

[7] To support my view, each year I have calculated the prospective rates of return for the 30 stocks comprising the Dow Jones Industrial Average (DJIA). This prospective return can be expressed as the sum of the dividend yield of each stock plus the expected long-term growth rate of the dividend, as estimated by Wall Street securities analysts. The prospective return for the DJIA is simply the average prospective return for the 30 constituent stocks. Each year-end period I calculate the risk premium as the difference between the prospective return for the DJIA and the long-term Treasury bond rate. My calculations reveal that risk premiums expanded sharply in the late 1970s from their very low levels during the late 1960s.

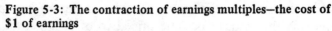

Figure 5-3: The contraction of earnings multiples—the cost of $1 of earnings

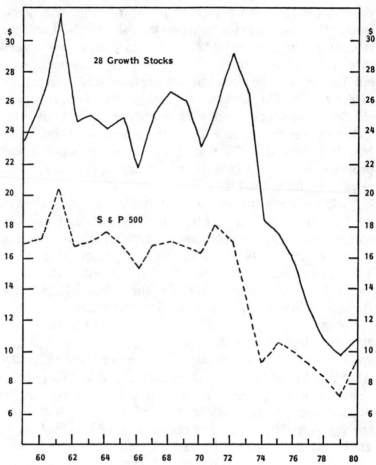

shown in Figure 5-2 was close to 30. At the start of 1980 it had fallen to less than 10. It was the decline in multiples that prevented stock prices from reflecting the real underlying progress most companies made in earnings and dividend growth. To be sure, this increase in risk premiums was related to inflation, which made all long-term investment decisions

93

more uncertain. But the result of these increased risk premiums was that stocks became priced to offer larger anticipated rates of return to attract investors. While the falling stock prices associated with increased risk premiums reduced rates of return over the past several years (and, in fact, caused substantial losses, depending on the investment period covered), such price declines tend to increase investment returns in the future. This leads to a somewhat paradoxical conclusion: because stocks were such a poor investment over the 70s, they should produce far more generous returns in the 80s. It is precisely the poor performance of equities that provided the price adjustments necessary to provide greater rates of return in the future.

Well, what returns are likely from here on out? First of all, I should point out that were it not for the drop in multiples, even the 1970s would have produced reasonable returns. If, for example, you could have bought stocks in 1968 at 1980's multiples, your total rate of return would have been in the 12 to 15 percent range. For the 1980s, I believe that the rate of return will be at least 15 to 18 percent.

Let me illustrate with AT&T—not because I think it's particularly attractive but because it is typical of the high prospective rates of return available from even our dullest stocks. At the end of 1980 AT&T had a dividend yield of somewhat better than 10 percent. That yield grew at a rate of 7½ percent over the last decade. A 1980 survey of Wall Street analysts revealed that they expected AT&T's dividend to grow at a 5½ to 6 percent rate. (This is a conservative estimate. It implies a nominal growth rate less than expected inflation. It gives no credit for the company's multibillion dollars of investment each year. The estimate is probably colored by the recent recession.) Suppose the dividend grows at only a bit better than 5½ percent. The total rate of return will then turn out to be approximately 16 percent. However, any relief from the prevailing mood of uncertainty and pessimism that led to a rise in multiples could bring spectacular

94

returns—even to a staid "widow's and orphan's" stock like AT&T.

What about the rest of the market? It abounds with golden eggs. I've done similar calculations for the 30 stocks of the Dow Jones Industrial Average. When you add the dividend yields for each stock to the long-run growth rates, the prospective return is approximately 15 to 18 percent. This average return of 15-18 percent looks good either by historical equity standards or in comparison to the 13-14 percent return available from Treasury bonds in 1980-81. My belief in the reasonable efficiency of markets leads me inevitably to the conclusion that, over the long pull, volatile common stocks are priced to yield more than top-quality, fixed-income securities.

I think that a good "maybe" is that panic-depressive institutional investors have gone too far in discounting the risks to our economic system. As I read the political news in the United States today, I see a country moving in a conservative direction and with a better understanding of the need for tax relief to encourage business investment and savings to get the country moving again.

Given the recent speculation in such areas as office buildings and farmland, stocks today still appear dirt cheap in an investment market where almost everything else is fully priced. Some institutions have developed an edifice complex—selling stocks at 5 times earnings in order to buy buildings at 15-20 times earnings. But the profitability of corporations is no worse than that of buildings—and the political risks are no less with real estate than with corporations. Many high-quality stocks are available at prices below book value and well below the replacement value of their assets. I think the analysis presented here leads inexorably to the conclusion that the major risk for investors at the start of the 1980s is the risk of being out of the market, not the risk of being in it.

6

Inflation and the Stock Market

by

Franco Modigliani
and
Richard A. Cohn

INFLATION AND THE STOCK MARKET

by Franco Modigliani
and Richard A. Cohn

This paper discusses the authors' recent research into the effect of inflation on the value of corporate equity. This work stemmed from an attempt to understand the causes of the substantial decline in price-earnings ratios in the United States over the period from the mid-1960s to the present, a period characterized by volatile and rising inflation.

Our research grew out of a broader study concerned with understanding the impact of high and variable inflation on the economy in general and on the financial markets in particular. In the course of that study we came to realize that one of the serious problems which inflation creates in an economy not accustomed to deal with it arises from the very real difficulties inflation introduces into the making of valid, rational economic and financial calculations. These considerations alerted us to the possibility that the puzzling dismal performance of the stock market might have arisen from errors of valuation produced by inflation. We were led to conjecture that the market might be making two distinct errors, both of which would result in a serious undervaluation of equity values. One would cause an undervaluation of profits, and the other would cause a serious upward bias in the rate at which those earnings were capitalized. Both of these errors could be traced to the effect of inflation in increasing nominal interest rates.

In the course of 1978 we designed a set of tests of this hypothesis based on a time-series or intertemporal analysis of the behavior of the Standard & Poor's 500 Stock Index in relation to inflation and other relevant variables. These tests are discussed in more detail below. Their results, which were published in spring 1979, appeared to support fully our hypothesis and to account for the observed behavior of the market in the course of recent inflation.[1] The results also suggested that, had equity values been rationally appraised, they would have been not far from twice as high as they then were.

Since that time we have been engaged in a second study, designed in part to respond to a variety of criticisms which were provoked by our original study. The second study is based on a comparative analysis of the behavior of stocks of individual companies. This approach has permitted us to deal with issues which could not be adequately resolved by the method of our first study. The results of the second study, which are also reported below, appear to lend further credence to our hypothesis.

The undervaluation hypothesis

In the past 12 to 15 years, U.S. stock prices, as measured by broad-based market indexes, have been roughly stagnant in nominal terms, while the general price level has more than doubled. This relationship is shown in Figure 6-1. Series 1 depicts stock prices, as measured by Standard & Poor's Industrials, and series 2 portrays general prices, as measured by the gross domestic product deflator for the 1968-79 period.

This phenomenon is not accounted for by a decline in aftertax profitability. This can be seen by comparing series 2 with the behavior of an estimate of aggregate profits for the nonfinancial corporate sector, fully corrected for the measurement biases induced by inflation, which is shown by series 3 in Figure 6-1. Generally speaking, profits have kept up with inflation, at least in recent years.

The profit series reported in Figure 6-1 is obtained by adjusting reported profits for three types of inflation dis-

---

[1] Franco Modigliani and Richard A. Cohn, "Inflation, Rational Valuation, and the Market," *Financial Analysts Journal,* March-April 1979.

100

Figure 6-1

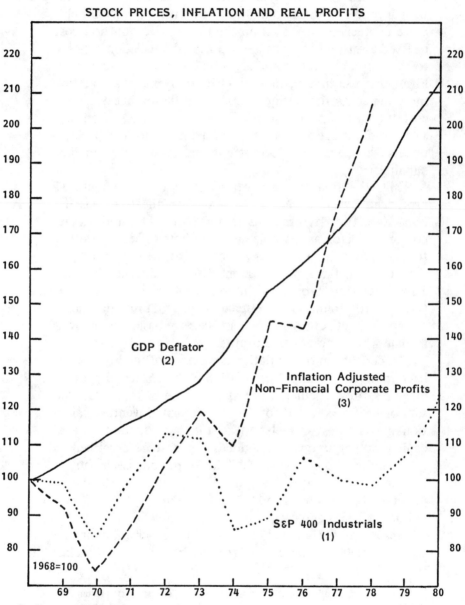

STOCK PRICES, INFLATION AND REAL PROFITS

In all cases, 1968 = 100.
Series 1: Standard & Poor's 400 Industrial Index.
Series 2: Gross domestic product deflator.
Series 3: Inflation-adjusted nonfinancial corporate profits.

101

tortions. The first has to do with depreciation, the second with inventory profits, and the third with interest on debt. Since depreciation is based on the historical acquisition cost of fixed assets, inflation causes reported depreciation expense to be an understatement of actual capital consumption. Firms that use first-in, first-out (FIFO) inventory accounting show paper profits during periods of inflation because their cost of goods sold understates the cost of replacing inventory. The third distortion results from a failure to add back to profits the gain from the real depreciation of monetary liabilities.

While the first two distortions serve to make reported profits an overstatement of true profits, the third has the opposite effect. It turns out that for the U.S. nonfinancial corporate sector as a whole, these effects offset each other to a considerable extent. As a result, reported earnings represent a reasonable approximation to fully adjusted earnings.[2] This conclusion is of some interest because it suggests that there is little foundation to the argument that inflation raises the corporate tax burden because taxes are based on reported income which exceeds true profits.

The conclusion that inflation-adjusted profitability has not been noticeably hurt by inflation is confirmed by other measures. In particular, total aftertax return to capital—the sum of profits adjusted for depreciation and inventory valuation plus interest—in relation to the reproduction cost of capital or corporate value added, can best be described as trendless over the post-World War II period. Even though inflation is currently high by U.S. historical standards, profitability is no worse now than it was during the bull market of the 1950s and early 1960s.

Because of the gradual erosion of real stock prices in the face of largely unchanged real profits, the rise in inflation has

---

[2] The net effect of the three distortions will, of course, vary substantially among firms.

102

been accompanied by a remarkable decline in the average price-earnings ratio, so that it is now less than half as large as it was in the late 1960s. A similar phenomenon has been observed in many other countries during this period of world-wide inflation.

This observation, which runs conspicuously counter to the traditional view that equities are hedges against inflation, raised in our minds the question of whether there might be a causal connection between the rise in inflation and the decline in price-earnings ratios (or, equivalently, the rise in earnings-price ratios).

One may first ask whether the observed positive association between earnings-price ratios and inflation can be attributed to rational investors' behavior. After all, it is a well-known and widely observed phenomenon that interest rates do rise roughly in step with inflation. The reason is that debt instruments have a value fixed in nominal terms whose purchasing power is eroded by inflation. Hence, interest rates tend to incorporate an inflation premium which maintains unchanged the "real interest rate," that is, the difference between the nominal interest rate and the rate of inflation. But it is a well-known proposition in the theory of rational equity valuation that the capitalization rate for earnings (the earnings-price ratio) should behave like the real rate of interest, that is, it should not change with inflation—except insofar as inflation changes the real interest rate itself (or the risk premium required by investors). The reason why the earnings-price ratio should behave like the real rate of interest instead of responding to inflation in the same way as nominal interest rates, is that equities, in contrast to debt, represent a claim on real assets and on the resulting real profit stream, which is, presumably, not significantly affected by inflation. Therefore, the earnings-price ratio can be viewed as the investor's real rate of return—analogous to the real rate of interest on debt. His nominal return will consist of the earnings-price ratio plus the rise in the price of stock in re-

103

sponse to the inflation-induced rise in nominal profits. This nominal appreciation of the asset performs the same function as the inflation premium component of interest rates.

These considerations led us to conjecture that the behavior of the market could reflect the mistaken view that a stock should be priced so as to produce an earnings-price ratio commensurate with the nominal rate of interest. Our suspicion was reinforced by a number of considerations, including the following: (1) Casual observation of the negative association between market action and interest rate movements, (2) The consideration that the association of earnings-price ratios and interest rates is consistent with rational behavior in the absence of inflation, for then changes in the nominal rate are in fact changes in the real rate. We thought it plausible that the market could be carrying over into an unaccustomed inflationary environment a behavior which had been appropriate for a long time, but was no longer so, (3) Perusal of the financial press, including brokerage house memorandums, and conversations with portfolio managers, which pointed in the direction of our conjecture.

We also hypothesized that there might be a further reason why inflation affected stock prices adversely—namely, a failure to properly correct profits for the gains from the inflation-induced depreciation of monetary liabilities. This failure means that the rise in interest rates due to inflation premiums results in a fictitious decline in observed profits. In this area too we observed a good deal of erroneous thinking as to whether a correction to profits was called for. It was argued, for example, that this gain from depreciation of debt should not be included in profits because it was a windfall gain rather than income, or because it did not represent a cash inflow.

To be sure, the correction for the depreciation of the debt, as indicated earlier, is but one of three corrections to reported earnings which should be made in the presence of inflation to obtain a true measurement. But we became convinced that the need for the adjustment for depreciation and inventories was on the whole broadly appreciated by investors. Thus we concluded that the failure to make the monetary liabilities adjustment was not compensated by errors in the opposite direction but was likely instead to result in a significant net downward bias. We were struck in this connection by the fact that even the prestigious national income accounts of the United States (and not only the United States) conscientiously make the two downward adjustments but fail to make the upward correction for the depreciation of monetary liabilities.

Time-series tests

In an effort to test our twin hypotheses, we related (by regression analysis) the behavior of a measure of the price-earnings ratio to the behavior of a measure of interest rates and inflation for the period 1953-77. The measure of price was the Standard & Poor's 500 Stock Index. The measure of earnings was earnings per share of the index, with an estimated adjustment for the depreciation and inventory valuation biases. Further auxiliary variables were utilized to correct current earnings for cyclical and other biases so as to approximate "noise-free" earnings.

Our review of the principles of rational valuation implies that the price-earnings ratio should respond inversely to the real rate of interest, that is, to the *difference* between the nominal rate of interest and the rate of inflation. This means that increases in the nominal interest rate and in inflation should both affect the price-earnings ratio significantly, but in a largely offsetting fashion—the first reducing it, the second increasing it. Thus, if in a given period the nominal rate should increase, say, 10 percent, but inflation increases as much, then the P/E should not change. Actually, because our measure of profits was not adjusted for the gains from depreciation of the debt, the positive effect of inflation should more than offset the negative effect of interest rates. Put differently, with an unchanged real rate inflation should increase the ratio of price to a measure of earnings which is understated by not incorporating the gain from the depreciation of the debt.

On the other hand, if there are valuation errors of the type we hypothesize, the effect of inflation should be less positive than under rational valuation. In the limit, if P/Es were controlled exclusively by nominal interest rates and profits were not corrected for the gain from debt, then the effect of inflation would be zero.

The results of our test were striking. The model was successful in accounting, quite closely, for the behavior of the price-earnings ratio throughout the period. The coefficient of inflation was close to zero; in fact, it was modestly *negative*. These findings are inconsistent with rational valuation and strongly supportive of both our hypotheses.

The results also provide a basis for assessing the quantitative effect of the valuation error on prices. We find that every percentage point increase in the steady-state inflation rate causes expected profits to fall by 5 percent and the capitalization rate to rise by 8 percent. Thus, every 1 percent increase in the long-run expected rate of inflation causes stock prices to fall by 13 percent in relation to true profits. Assuming that a permanent rate of inflation of 6-7 percent was anticipated at the end of 1977, stock prices at that time were undervalued on the order of 50 percent. We suspect that the level of undervaluation is not very different at present.

Criticism

Our hypothesis that market participants are making systematic errors in valuation has, not surprisingly, provoked a good deal of uneasiness on the part of our academic colleagues and the investment community and has elicited a fair amount of criticism.

One criticism is that it is not appropriate to treat the inflation premium component of interest as part of profit because it is not part of cash flow and is therefore not available for

106

distribution to shareholders. Two responses are in order. First, leverage measured as the ratio of net debt to the reproduction cost of corporate assets appears to be stable for the nonfinancial corporate sector. Such stability implies that corporations have tended to refinance the repayment of principal induced by the inflation premium, thereby restoring the cash which they would otherwise have lost because of that premium. Second, since cash flow is conventionally defined as profit after taxes plus noncash charges, this component of interest payments is part of cash flow because it is properly part of aftertax profits. It is a repayment of real principal and should no more be treated as a deduction from cash flow than any other principal repayment.

Another criticism we have received is that, at most, only part of the inflation premium component of interest should be added to conventionally measured profits because the inflation gain that accrues to the debtor corporation is offset by a corresponding loss to the corporate pension plan. This loss in the final analysis falls on the corporation as the de facto guarantor of the promises made by its pension plan to beneficiaries.

Here we must distinguish between the effect of anticipated inflation fully reflected in interest rates and the effect of unanticipated inflation. With respect to the former, inflation does not benefit debtors, for the debt devaluation precisely offsets the higher interest they pay. Thus the corporate debtor does not gain. By the same token, the creditor pension plan does not lose. In this case, therefore, there is only a downward bias in reported corporate income if one fails to add the inflation premium to profits. And, it might be noted, there is a corresponding upward bias in the pension plan's income if it treats interest entirely as current income rather than as partly a compensation for loss of real principal.

Unanticipated inflation, by contrast, is a source of real gain to the debtor insofar as it results in his paying a rate of interest below the current market rate and possibly negative in real terms. This gain is, to some extent, offset for the entire corporate sector by the loss accruing to the creditor pension plans, though the extent of this offset would vary from firm to firm. However, these windfall gains and losses have nothing to do with the correction of profits for gains on monetary liabilities which we have advocated. To be sure, to the extent that fully corrected profits reflect some windfall gains but fail to reflect the corresponding windfall losses of corporate pension plans, there would be some ground for expected profits to be below actual profits, justifying some decline in the ratio of price to adjusted earnings. But this effect could explain no more than a small portion of the observed decline in the overall price-earnings ratios.

Yet another criticism has dealt with our model of equity valuation, which employs an earnings capitalization approach. We have been told that investors actually use a dividend discounting approach, and since dividends are simply dividends, an error in measuring profits can have no effect on valuation. But earnings capitalization and dividend discounting approaches to valuation should be consistent. Therefore, there must be something wrong with this argument. The difficulty is that expected future dividends must relate to expectations concerning the amount of earnings retained and reinvested; since retained earnings are the difference between total earnings and dividends, an underestimate of earnings leads to an underestimate of expected future dividends.

Perhaps the most challenging criticisms we have received are those which argue that inflation has produced a systematic, rationally warranted change in the price-earnings ratio. One of these criticisms argues that inflation has somehow reduced expected earnings relative to current earnings, specifically by reducing the anticipated real growth rate of corporate profits. Another holds that the rise in inflation has coincided with a rise in the risk premium that stock market investors require, perhaps because of oil price shocks, perhaps because of a climate unfavorable to business, perhaps because inflation itself has produced a new element of uncertainty in the economy, even if irrationally. The validity of these two criticisms cannot easily be ruled out by means of time-series analysis because, while inflation can be directly measured, our critics have not offered an explicit measure of profit expectations or risk. However, some tests can be made by means of a comparative analysis of the values of individual stocks during the inflationary experience since the mid-1960s. Our attempt to apply this method is described below.

Cross-sectional analysis

The hypothesis of a rising market risk premium, which can be referred to as the Risk Premium Explanation (RPE), can be usefully illustrated by means of the graph in Figure 6-2. The vertical axis represents the required real rate of return as measured by the earnings-price ratio. Along the horizontal axis we measure the risk of individual stocks in terms of the well-known beta coefficient of the capital asset market model, as developed by Sharpe and others.[3] The lower upward-sloping solid line depicts the mid-1960s relationship between beta and the earnings-price ratio.

The intercept of this market line corresponds to the real (aftertax) interest rate, and the line rises since the required return increases with risk. The height of the line corresponding to a beta of one represents the average earnings-price ratio prevailing in the mid-1960s. Between the mid-1960s and the present the average earnings-price ratio roughly doubled, as shown by the upper horizontal dashed line, which represents the current level.

Any explanation of this current market earnings-price ratio must produce a market line which goes through the intersection of the higher dashed horizontal line and the vertical dashed line corresponding to a beta equal to unity. According to the MCH, the new market line can be approximated by the upper rising solid line. This is because the MCH

---

[3] W. F. Sharpe, "Capital Asset Price: The Theory of Market Equilibrium under Conditions of Risk," *Journal of Finance*, September 1964.

Figure 6-2: Alternative explanations of the collapse in price-earnings ratios since the mid-1960s

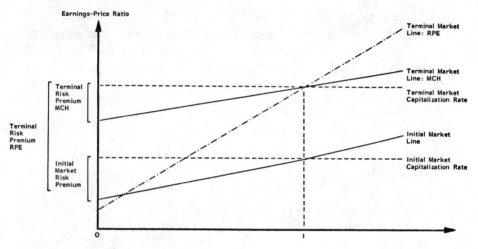

RPE: Risk premium explanation.
MCH: Modigliani-Cohn hypothesis.

attributes the change in the average earnings-price ratio to the fact that the inflation-induced rise in interest rates has produced an across-the-board rise in the required rate of return quite independently of the initial beta. If so, the market line must have shifted roughly parallel to its original position and the change in the average earnings-price ratio must be roughly the same as the rise in the intercept.

By contrast, according to the RPE, the new market line can be represented by something like the dotted dashed line. Indeed, according to this view, the intercept was initially and still remains the real aftertax rate of interest as called for by rational valuation. As that rate has actually fallen since the mid-1960s, the new intercept is somewhat lower than that of the original market line. The position of the market line is now fixed by that point and by the fact that it must go through the average earnings-price ratio at a beta of one. Thus, while earnings-price ratios for low-beta stocks should have been largely unchanged, those for high-beta stocks

110

should have increased substantially, enough to account for the increase in the average earnings-price ratio.

These alternative hypotheses have very different implications as to what should account for the change in the P/Es of individual stocks in the course of each period. The RPE suggests that there should have been little change in P/E for low-risk stocks and larger and larger declines for stocks characterized by high-beta risk. In other words, it is the high-beta stocks that are responsible for the decline in the average. We should thus observe a strong negative correlation between the change in price-earnings ratio and the beta of the stock.

According to the MCH, by contrast, there should be a clear negative association between the proportional change in the price-earnings ratio of a stock and its initial price-earnings ratio. The reason for this proposition is that the lower the initial earnings-price ratio, the larger the proportional increase that an increment to earnings-price ratios of a given amount represents and therefore the larger the proportional decline in P/E. To illustrate this point, suppose stock A had initially a P/E of 5, or an earnings-price ratio of 0.2, and stock B had a P/E of 20, or an earnings-price ratio of 0.05. Suppose further that because of inflation, interest rates rose by 500 basis points. According to the MCH, this would tend to increase all earnings-price ratios by that amount. For stock A, the earnings-price ratio would rise by one quarter, to 0.25, and the P/E would fall by 20 percent, to 4. For stock B, on the other hand, the earnings-price ratio would double, to 0.1, and the P/E would fall by 50 percent, a much greater decline than in the case of stock A. On the other hand, under the MCH one would not expect a significant relation between the change in the P/E and the initial beta.

In order to test these alternative hypotheses, we examined by means of regression analysis changes in price-earnings ratios in relation to the initial price-earnings ratio and beta for a sample of some 200 U.S. industrial corporations over the period from the end of 1968 to 1973, 1973 to 1978, and the entire decade 1968-78. These firms were selected with the help of E. F. Hutton & Company securities analysts from those which they actively followed. The performance of these samples roughly matched that of the S&P Industrials. We included as independent variables information on earnings growth expectations and the change in the dividend payout ratio in order to control for changes in expected real growth that should have affected price-earnings ratios. We also employed a leverage measure as an independent variable in order to test our hypothesis that the market fails to correct profits for the inflation premium component of interest.[4]

The results of our study are strikingly supportive of the MCH and counter to the implications of the RPE.[5] It is, indeed, stocks that started out with a high P/E that suffered the largest relative decline; the estimated increase in the intercept of the market line over the 1968-78 period is on the order of the increase in inflation and interest rates. At the same time, there is no evidence that the high-beta stocks experienced above-average declines, as suggested by the RPE. If anything, high-beta stocks tended to perform relatively better. Thus our results imply that there is absolutely no evidence that the decline in the market was due to a rise in the risk premium as related to beta. If anything, the market risk premium appears to have declined during the 1968-78 period.

Our test also throws some light on the view that the market decline can be attributed to a decline in anticipated profits or in their growth rate. To test this notion, we secured estimates of five-year expected growth in earnings per share for each firm at the beginning of each interval. Our sources were the Value Line Investment Survey and E. F. Hutton securities analysts. We find that there was only a modest decline in the anticipated real growth rate of earnings be-

---

[4] The authors are deeply grateful to E. F. Hutton & Company, and particularly to Peter N. Smith of that firm, for providing us with much of the data that we required.

[5] The results are summarized in the appendix at the end of this chapter.

tween the beginning and end of the full period. In particular, there was essentially no change from the end of 1973 to the end of 1978, a period during which the average price-earnings ratio for the firms in our sample declined 36 percent.

Given rational valuation, one would have expected a noticeably positive relationship between leverage and the change in our measure of P/E, which was based on *reported* earnings not corrected for the effects of inflation. This is because the inflation premium component of interest increases with inflation, thus lowering reported earnings in relation to true earnings. But the observed relationship is actually negative, suggesting, as we had hypothesized on the basis of our time-series results, that leveraged firms are penalized by the market when interest rates rise in response to increases in expectations of inflation.

Conclusion

In summary, both our time-series and our cross-sectional results suggest that inflation, through its effect on nominal interest rates, has caused systematic valuation errors as a result of which stocks are at present seriously undervalued. The most undervalued shares appear to be those of firms characterized by relatively high price-earnings ratios, low betas, and high leverage.

What do our findings imply about the future course of stock prices? If the current historically low level of stock prices in relation to earnings is the result of a serious inflation-induced valuation error, as we have hypothesized and have endeavored to document, then this level cannot last indefinitely. Indeed, this is precisely what we mean by saying that equities are "undervalued." We mean that, provided earnings continue to keep up with inflation, as it seems only reasonable to expect, then current P/Es cannot endure. The reason is that a continuation of the current P/Es implies a return from equities so disproportionally high in relation to

113

the return from bonds and other fixed-rate instruments that investors could not fail to recognize that the market was seriously undervalued and to respond accordingly.

To illustrate this point, even after the rise in stock prices in 1980 the average earnings-price ratio for the S&P 500 was around 12 percent. With the rate of inflation running around 10 percent, a constant P/E implies a 10 percent rise in stock prices on this account alone, and thus a total nominal rate of return of 22 percent. This compares with a return on corporate bonds of about 14-15 percent in late 1980.

But the differential is even more dramatic on an aftertax basis, which is the relevant one. For equities, the only portion of the 22 percent return subject to income tax is the dividend, which amounts to some 5 percent. Assuming a representative marginal tax rate of 40 percent, the aftertax real return of equities would come to 10 percent. One must also allow for the effect of the capital gains tax, which is harder to estimate because of its deferrability. A reasonable guess of its present value might be perhaps 150 basis points, leaving a net real return of roughly 8½ percent. For corporate bonds, on the other hand, a similar calculation yields a real aftertax return of minus 2 percent. An alternative calculation based on tax-exempt bonds yields a slightly higher return of plus 1 percent. A differential of this magnitude between stocks and bonds, if maintained, cannot fail to induce investors to shift the composition of their portfolios in the direction of equities, thus bidding up equity prices until P/Es have moved back (or possibly snapped back) to a level consistent with rational valuation.

Even though P/Es could not stabilize without setting the stage for significant recovery, one can conceive of an alternative scenario in which, as in recent years, P/Es tend to sag. For when P/Es decline, the undervaluation implicit in unduly large earnings-price ratios is hidden from investors as the high return from earnings is offset, possibly more than offset, by the capital loss resulting from the sinking price.

How likely is this alternative scenario? In terms of our

114

hypothesis of irrational behavior, this could only happen if the rate of inflation continued to increase steadily over the coming years. While it is not our purpose here to evaluate the probability of such a trend, we would like to note that even if nominal interest rates should continue to rise under the spur of rising inflation, a further decline in P/Es is not inevitable. We have shown that such a decline is the result of irrational inflation illusion. We believe it entirely possible that the market may gradually learn to see through inflation fallacies—even without the benefit of reading our papers. Indeed, one might interpret recent market action as supporting this hopeful belief. To conclude, one can see many reasons why—before too long—the market should stage a healthy recovery toward the much higher level called for by rational valuation. But anyone who pursues an investment policy based on rational valuation in a world in which lapses from rationality seem to have a way of persisting does so at his peril.

APPENDIX

In the equations reported below (in Exhibit A-1), which are representative of those we obtained in our cross-sectional study, the dependent variable is the change in the logarithm of the price-earnings ratio.

The sample size represents the number of firms for which all of the relevant information was available.

The critical coefficients from the standpoint of our hypothesis are those of P/x and D_0. The absolute values of the coefficients of P/x represent estimates of the increase, measured as a decimal, in the intercept of the market line referred to in the text. The reported estimates of the coefficients for the two time periods are somewhat larger than the corresponding increases in interest rates, but these estimates are probably upward-biased, primarily because of the general tendency of price-earnings ratios to regress toward the mean. After correcting for this bias, we estimate the increase in the

Exhibit A-1

Time period	Number of observations	Independent variable	Estimated coefficient	t = statistic	Mean value
1968-73	177	a_0	-.066	-0.54	
		P/x	-.032	-2.41	20.67
		D_0	-.027	-2.32	2.74
		$\beta \cdot P/x$	.012	1.21	21.59
		$\dot{d} - \dot{\pi}$	.543	4.02	- 0.28
		$\dot{x} \cdot P/x$	.025	5.00	9.32
		$(g_1 - g_0)P/x$	.001	1.90	- 2.73
1973-78	175	a_0	.158	3.56	
		P/x	-.043	-7.12	17.86
		D_0	-.020	-3.02	2.62
		$\beta \cdot P/x$	.010	2.13	18.82
		$\dot{d} - \dot{\pi}$	.286	4.93	0.01
		$(g_1 - g_0)P/x$	.0004	1.93	33.66

Where

a_0 = Constant term
P = Initial price per share
x = Weighted average of initial earnings and dividend per share
D_0 = Initial ratio of net debt to earnings
β = Equity beta
$\dot{d} - \dot{\pi}$ = Change in logarithm of dividend payout ratio over the period
$\dot{x}$ = Change in logarithm of x over the period
$g_1 - g_0$ = Change in expected percentage growth in x over the period

intercept of the market line to be .025 and .033 over the 1968-73 and 1973-78 periods, respectively.

The other coefficients of interest, those of the leverage variable, D_0, should be positive according to rational valuation. As indicated in the text, however, and as shown, their estimated values are negative.

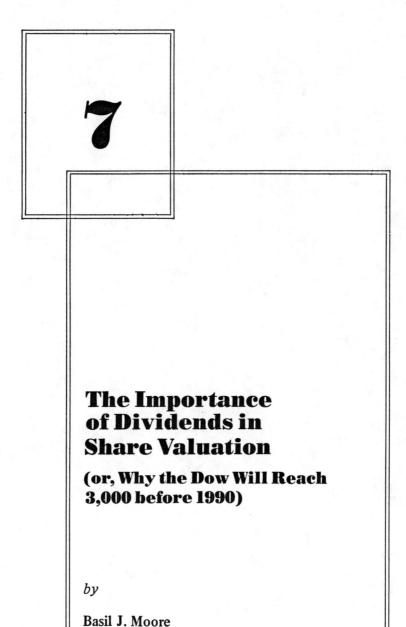

7

The Importance of Dividends in Share Valuation

(or, Why the Dow Will Reach 3,000 before 1990)

by

Basil J. Moore

THE IMPORTANCE OF DIVIDENDS IN SHARE VALUATION (OR, WHY THE DOW WILL REACH 3,000 BEFORE 1990)

by Basil J. Moore

> *Watching for riches consumeth the flesh and the care thereof driveth away sleep.*
>
> *Ecclesiastes 30:24*

Once upon a time (back in the 1960s) it was widely believed that sensible investors should buy common stocks for their generous returns and protection against inflation. Their annual historical long-run nominal total return was calculated at about 10 percent, well above the long-run inflation rate. However, over the past decade, as the rate of inflation has accelerated, the real value of shares has fallen dramatically. The Dow Jones Industrial Average, which was about 900 at the end of the 1960s, ended the decade of the 1970s still languishing around the 900 mark. Since reaching their peak level in 1968, share values in real terms have fallen by approximately 50 percent. The nominal return of common stocks has been only about 5 percent, well below the inflation rate. During the 1970s common stocks fared worse than virtually all other investment assets—including gold, stamps, old masters, and houses. Nor has the U.S. experience been unique. Since 1969 the real value of shares has fallen in most countries where major stock exchanges exist.

What explains this dismal performance of stocks over the past decade? Why in virtually all countries have equities not served to protect wealth owners from the ravages of inflation? After all, shares represent indirect ownership claims to

121

real business wealth. As such, their value was long expected to rise—like that of residential real estate—with movements in the general price level.

The most common explanation for the recent negative relationship between share values and inflation is that after-tax corporate profits in real terms have been adversely affected by inflation. Increases in the price of imported energy and other raw materials, and increases in money wages in excess of gains in average labor productivity, must be passed on in higher prices if profits are not to be squeezed. Lags in the markup process as the rate of inflation has accelerated, plus the lower levels of capacity utilization induced by government's largely unsuccessful attempts to restrain cost-induced inflation by restrictive demand management means, are widely accepted explanations for the fall in corporate profitability. A rising tax share due to inflation is frequently adduced as a supplementary explanation for the fall in aftertax profits.

Many researchers have analyzed the effects of inflation on company profitability. In a widely cited paper, Nordhaus concluded that gross profit rates had fallen since 1965.[1] However, on reexamining the data, Feldstein and Summers found little statistical support for a negative trend after adjusting for capacity utilization.[2] Similarly, Holland and Myers recently found no empirical evidence for a negative trend in aftertax rates of return, though a dummy for the 1970s indicated that the average return was 1.5 percent lower during this period.[3]

None of the above estimates, however, were concerned with the rate of return to shareholders, who, theory suggests,

[1] W. Nordhaus, "The Falling Share of Profits," *Brookings Papers on Economic Activity*, no. 1, 1974.

[2] M. Feldstein and L. Summers, "Is the Rate of Profit Falling?" *Brookings Papers on Economic Activity*, no. 1, 1977.

[3] D. Holland and S. Myers, "Trends in Corporate Profitability and Capital Costs," in *The Nation's Capital Needs: Three Studies* (New York: Committee for Economic Development, 1979).

should gain at the expense of bondholders during periods of rising inflation. Calculation of the return to shareholders is extremely sensitive to the accounting conventions adopted. Inflation necessarily alters the valuation of business assets and liabilities. Such valuation changes produce accompanying capital gains and losses, most of which prevailing accounting conventions disregard.

As is now widely recognized, there are several reasons why reported earnings represent an overstatement of "true" profits in an inflationary environment. First, historical cost depreciation results in an underestimate of replacement cost depreciation under inflation. As a result, depreciation reserves are insufficient to replace existing assets, so that expenses are understated and reported income represents an overestimate. Second, to the extent that inventory accounting is based on first-in, first-out (FIFO) rather than last-in, first-out (LIFO) conventions, income is overstated. Reported profits are inflated due to the inclusion in income of nominal capital gains on inventories whenever prices are rising, even though the inventories sold must be restored at higher replacement costs.

While the above are the adjustments conventionally highlighted, in order to determine shareholder income additional adjustments must be made to incorporate fully all the capital gains or losses associated with inflation. Most important, inflation reduces the real value of financial assets and liabilities denominated in money terms. Current accounting conventions ignore this fact insofar as such gains are unrealized. It is well known that bondholders suffer from inflation. The counterpart of the bondholders' loss is the bond issuers' gain. The net worth of shareholders is thus increased due to the depreciation of the real purchasing power of their net financial liabilities. Nonfinancial corporations are substantial net debtors. Since the net financial liabilities of nonfinancial corporations are currently about $500 billion, shareholder profits rise by roughly $5 billion for every 1 percent increase in the inflation rate. In 1979, with an inflation rate of 13 percent, this amounted to $65 billion.

As inflation comes to be generally anticipated, nominal interest rates rise to compensate lenders for the expected depreciation in the real value of their loans. These higher interest rates paid by firms are conventionally fully deducted in firm income accounts as a current expense. However, the offsetting depreciation in the real value of the firm's debts due to inflation is disregarded. It is only the real cost of borrowing, the excess of nominal interest expense over the inflation-induced gains due to the lower real value of the firm's liabilities, that is properly considered the current cost of debt liabilities.

Two other adjustments are somewhat more controversial. When the replacement cost of capital goods rises by more or less than the general price level, there is a case for entering a capital gain or loss to reflect the differential inflation rate of capital goods. This follows since the real value of shareholders' equity is then higher or lower. Second, a rise in market interest rates will reduce the current market value of the firm's outstanding net financial liabilities. The case can be made that since such capital changes increase the real value of shareholder net worth, they should also be included in shareholder current income. This reflects the fact that companies, and hence their shareholders, gain from having issued debt securities before a rise in interest rates occurs.

A number of economists have recently attempted to estimate inflation-adjusted profits to shareholders.[4] Their studies show that inflation-induced gains and losses greatly affect profits accruing to shareholders. This adds to the uncertainty over the effects of inflation on profit rates, since there is no consensus as to the correct adjustments to use. In an inflationary environment neither managers nor shareholders know with certainty what proprietors' "true" profits really are. But it is accurate to conclude that after all the appropriate inflation adjustments have been made, there is no evidence that

---

[4] These studies have been summarized in P. Cagan and R. Lipsey, *The Financial Effects of Inflation* (Cambridge, Mass.: Ballinger Publishing, 1978).

aftertax rates of return to shareholders have fallen over the last decade as the rate of inflation has accelerated.

It has been increasingly recognized that the accounting profession's resistance to including recurrent though unrealized gains and losses due to inflation in the profit and loss statements of business firms, because of firm dictates of accounting prudence not to recognize such gains until they are realized, involves an important departure from realism. It remains to be seen how the new inflation-adjusted data mandated by the Financial Accounting Standards Board (FASB) will be received. One problem is that the FASB has required two different versions of inflation adjustment—constant dollar accounting, which adjusts for changes in the consumer price index, and current cost accounting, which involves estimating the current cost of company assets. There is considerable controversy within the accounting profession over which method produces the more meaningful results.

If the previous argument is accepted, it leads to somewhat of a paradox. If real net aftertax profits accruing to shareholders, when expressed as a return on corporate equity at replacement cost and fully adjusted for all gains and losses due to inflation, have not in fact fallen secularly as the rate of inflation has risen over the past decade, why have share values not also kept pace with inflation? Remember, S&P's 500 Stock Index in 1979 was slightly lower than in 1968, while the consumer price index had doubled.

Unfortunately, little agreement exists at present among economists as to the explanation for this collapse of share values. Feldstein stresses tax factors, in particular the double taxation of dividends and the differential treatment of dividend and capital gains income. Malkiel has attributed the decline in share valuation to an increase in the risk premium required on equities due to the greater uncertainty surrounding profits in an inflationary world.[5] It is true that the confidence and optimism of the early 1960s was replaced by a

_____
[5] See Chapter 5.

mood of anxiety and foreboding in the 1970s. Yet there is no hard evidence of a rise in yield spreads between new-issue yields on Treasury bonds and the total return on equities. Hendershott has suggested that the decline in share values may be due to the favorable tax treatment of housing, which has increased its attraction as an investment for households.[6] Alternatively, Modigliani and Cohn have been reluctantly driven to the conclusion that the capital markets are "irrationally" undervaluing equities by roughly 50 percent, due to the omission of the decline in the real value of corporate debt from conventional profit estimates.[7]

One of Irving Fisher's central premises was that the value of financial assets at any point in time depended solely on the discounted sum of their future cash flows to the holder.[8] The idea that present share values are the value of future prospects discounted at an appropriate rate is now standard in every finance text. However, there is considerable disagreement as to whether it is future dividends, future earnings, or future market values that are the appropriate definitions of future prospects.

In a widely cited and extremely influential article, Modigliani and Miller (M&M) have argued that it is immaterial whether shares are viewed as the discounted value of future dividends or of future net earnings generated by the firm.[9] Properly defined, both the future stream of dividends and the future stream of earnings are entirely equivalent.

While there is no doubt that the M&M "dividend irrelevance" theorem is logically correct, it is critically dependent on its assumptions. In order to isolate the effects of dividend policy, M&M assume that both future earnings and future investment expenditures are predetermined and independent

[6] P. Hendershott, "The Decline in Aggregate Share Values: Inflation and Taxation of the Return from Equities and Owner-Occupied Housing," Working Paper no. 370, National Bureau of Economic Research, July 1979.

[7] See Chapter 6.

[8] I. Fisher, *The Theory of Interest* (New York: Macmillan, 1930).

[9] M. Miller and F. Modigliani, "Dividend Policy, Growth, and the Valuation of Shares," *Journal of Business*, October 1961, pp. 411-32.

of dividend policy. As a result, any change in dividends paid out will necessarily involve an equal and offsetting change in new-share issues. The total value of the firm is then independent of its dividend policy.

However, in a world where corporations rely primarily on retentions rather than new issues to finance future investment spending, it is illegitimate to assume that future investment policy is independent of dividend policy. If, for example, the alternative extreme assumption were made that new issues are zero, which for most corporations is much closer to actual practice, dividend payout and future investment spending are necessarily inversely related.

Over the last decade, dividends paid out as a proportion of fully adjusted equity earnings have not remained constant, but have fallen sharply. Whether due to the increased uncertainty of true earnings under inflation or to the favorable tax treatment of capital gains income vis-à-vis dividend income, managers have chosen to reduce their payout ratios over the last decade. This implies that corporate retentions, and hence corporate investment (including merger spending), must have risen, since corporations are legally deterred from devoting their earnings to the repurchase of their own shares as a way of avoiding income tax.

The inflation-induced capital gains accruing to shareholder net worth as a result of the fall in the real value of corporate debt do not result in cash flows distributable to shareholders. They can only be realized to the extent that corporate managers are able to borrow to restore their debt ratios in real terms. In addition, managers must be willing to distribute the proceeds of such debt issue to their shareholders. Debt covenants currently preclude such distributions to protect company bondholders. But if these covenants were to be redefined in real rather than nominal terms, this problem would largely disappear.

If Fisher's hypothesis is taken seriously, the market capitalizes expected future dividend income to shareholders and not future earnings of the company. Moreover, in an inflationary environment it is the behavior of *real* dividends, not their nominal values, which will be relevant for investors with no money illusion. Table 7-1 presents the aggregate behavior of dividends per share paid on stocks in the S&P 500 index in nominal and constant dollars and their respective growth rates. As may be seen, after growing at an average compound rate of 4.8 percent over the period from 1946 to 1966, per share dividends in real terms have stopped growing and actually declined. The real value of per share dividends paid out in 1979 was 13 percent below their peak real value, in 1966.

As seen in Table 7-1, by 1965 the dividend yield had fallen to 3 percent, as a result of the high growth rate of real dividends experienced over the previous 20 years. Since then, the market has gradually adjusted its expected future growth rate of real dividends downward in line with their actual performance. In 1974 share values fell sharply, reflecting the rise in dividend yields and the 30 percent fall in price-dividend multiples. By 1979 the dividend yield had risen to 5.5 percent, a level unprecedented since the early 1950s. This near doubling (+82 percent) in the dividend yield was sufficient to cause price-dividend multiples to fall by nearly one half (−45 percent). However, dividends per share more than doubled (+113 percent), so that the share price index rose by 17 percent. Nevertheless, due to the rise in the price level, share values in real terms were virtually halved. Since real dividends fell by only 10 percent, this fall in real share values was due primarily to the rise in dividend yields.

The total real return on shares, R, may be expressed:

$$R \approx \frac{D}{S} + \left(\frac{\dot{S}}{P}\right) \approx \frac{D}{S} + \left(\frac{\dot{D}}{P}\right) + \left(\frac{\dot{S}}{D}\right)$$

where D/S is the dividend yield, S is the share price, P is the price index, and a dot over a variable represents the proportional rate of change in the variable with respect to time. In words, this equation states that the total real return is approximately equal to the sum of the dividend yield, the rate

128

of growth of real dividends, and the proportional change in the price-dividend multiple.

Efficient market theory implies that all public information is compounded in the present stock market price. In the short run, no one can predict future changes in the share price-dividend multiple, so the short-run expected value of $(\dot{S}/D)^e = 0$. As a result, the *expected* return on shares may be represented by the sum of the first two terms. If inflation reduces the real rate of dividend growth, so that $(\dot{D}/P)^e$ falls, share values will be depressed. The dividend yield will rise until the expected total return on equities has been restored to their reservation supply price. As the dividend yield, D/S, rises, $\dot{S}/D$ becomes negative, so that the total return to shareholders actually falls. In the short run, therefore, equities are always a very poor hedge against an accelerating inflation which lowers the expected growth rate of real dividends.

Over the longer run the dividend yield will gradually rise to compensate investors for the lower rate of growth of the real dividend stream. Though share values will be lower, and the resulting return on shares will be low and even negative, the expected long-run total return, $D/S + (\dot{D}/P)^e + (\dot{S}/D)^e$, should always approximate the reservation supply price of equity capital. It is for this reason that some commentators will always be optimistic regarding the future return expected on shares, no matter how deep the slump in share values.

There is, in fact, ample evidence that for selected stocks the current pessimism of the market has gone too far. Whenever share price-dividend multiples remain unchanged at their current levels, the total annual return is simply the sum of the current dividend yield and the expected future growth of dividends—above 15 percent. Only if future price-dividend multiples fall further will these total return expectations be disappointed. However, to satisfy the bears, current dividend yields could still go higher and price-dividend multiples lower, especially if inflation accelerates and the negative growth of real dividends continues. As shown in Table 7-1,

129

Table 7-1: Share values, inflation, and dividends

Year	Share values (S&P 500) (S) (1941-43 = 10)	Annual growth rate (percent)	CPI (1967=100) (P)	Annual growth rate (percent)	Real share values (S/P)	Annual growth rate (percent)	Dividend yield (S&P 500) (D/S)	Dividends per share (D) (D/S) × S = D	Annual growth rate (percent)	Real dividends (D/P)	Annual growth rate (percent)	Share price/dividend ratio (S/D)
1979	103.02	7.3	217.4	9.6	47.39	− 2.1	5.46	5.625	10.80	2.59	− 0.3	18.3
1978	96.02	− 2.2	198.4	9.3	48.39	−10.6	5.28	5.070	11.75	2.59	2.4	18.9
1977	98.20	− 3.7	181.5	6.5	54.10	− 9.6	4.62	4.537	17.86	2.50	10.6	21.6
1976	102.01	18.4	170.5	5.8	59.83	12.0	3.77	3.846	3.65	2.26	− 1.7	26.5
1975	86.16	4.0	161.2	9.1	53.45	− 4.7	4.31	3.713	0.27	2.30	− 8.4	23.2
1974	82.85	−22.9	147.7	11.0	56.09	−30.5	4.47	3.703	12.65	2.51	1.6	22.4
1973	107.43	− 1.6	133.1	6.2	80.71	7.4	3.06	3.287	5.98	2.47	− 0.4	32.7
1972	109.20	11.1	125.3	3.3	87.15	7.6	2.84	3.102	0.50	2.48	2.4	35.2
1971	98.29	18.1	121.3	4.3	81.03	13.2	3.14	3.086	− 3.17	2.54	7.3	31.8
1970	83.22	−14.9	116.3	5.9	71.56	−19.7	3.83	3.187	0.55	2.74	5.2	25.6
1969	97.84	− 0.9	109.8	5.4	89.11	− 5.9	3.24	3.170	4.62	2.89	− 0.3	30.0
1968	98.70	7.4	104.2	4.2	94.72	3.0	3.07	3.030	3.90	2.91	− 1.0	31.8
1967	91.93	7.8	100.0	2.9	91.93	4.8	3.20	2.942	1.48	2.94	1.3	30.5
1966	85.26	− 3.3	97.2	2.9	87.71	− 5.8	3.40	2.899	9.50	2.98	6.4	28.7
1965	88.17	8.4	94.5	1.7	93.30	6.5	3.00	2.645	8.00	2.80	6.1	33.3

Year												
1964	81.37	16.5	92.9	1.3	87.59	15.0	3.01	2.449	10.58	2.64	9.1	32.3
1963	69.87	12.0	91.7	1.2	76.19	10.7	3.17	2.215	5.36	2.42	4.3	31.5
1962	62.38	−5.9	90.6	1.1	68.85	−6.9	3.37	2.102	6.45	2.32	5.4	29.7
1961	66.27	18.7	89.6	1.0	73.96	17.5	2.98	1.975	1.90	2.20	0.9	33.6
1960	55.85	−2.7	88.7	1.6	62.97	−4.2	3.47	1.938	3.92	2.18	1.9	28.3
1959	57.38	24.1	87.3	0.8	65.73	23.1	3.23	1.865	1.58	2.14	0.9	30.6
1958	46.24	4.2	86.6	2.7	53.39	1.4	3.97	1.836	3.73	2.12	− 7.4	25.1
1957	44.38	−4.8	84.3	3.6	52.64	−8.1	4.35	1.930	1.20	2.29	− 2.1	23.0
1956	46.62	15.1	81.4	1.5	57.27	12.4	4.09	1.907	15.42	2.34	13.6	24.5
1955	40.49	36.4	80.2	− 0.4	50.49	36.9	4.08	1.652	12.38	2.06	12.6	24.6
1954	26.96	20.1	80.5	0.5	36.88	19.5	4.95	1.470	2.49	1.83	2.2	20.6
1953	24.73	0.9	80.1	0.8	30.87	0.2	5.80	1.434	0.91	1.79	0.0	17.7
1952	24.50	9.7	79.5	2.2	30.82	7.3	5.80	1.421	3.77	1.79	1.7	17.7
1951	22.34	21.4	77.8	7.9	28.71	12.6	6.13	1.369	13.28	1.76	4.8	16.3
1950	18.40	20.8	72.1	1.0	25.52	19.6	6.57	1.209	20.44	1.68	19.1	15.6
1949	15.23	− 1.9	71.4	− 1.0	21.33	− 1.0	6.59	1.004	12.49	1.41	12.8	15.1
1948	15.53	2.4	72.1	7.8	21.54	− 5.0	5.78*	0.898	15.34	1.25	7.7	17.3
1947	15.17	−11.2	66.9	14.4	22.67	−22.4	5.13*	0.778	14.76	1.16	0.0	19.5
1946	17.08	12.7	58.5	8.5	29.20	3.8	3.97*	0.678	6.75	1.16	− 1.7	25.4
1945	15.16	21.6	53.9	2.3	28.12	18.9	4.19*	0.635	5.90	1.18	3.5	24.0
1966-79		1.47		6.39		− 4.63			5.23		− 1.08	
1945-65		9.20		2.84		6.18			7.39		4.41	

*Moody's.

the postwar high for the dividend yield was 6.6 percent, with a price-dividend multiple of 15. The historic low for the price-dividend multiple on an annual basis was 12.7, in 1917. In 1932 it was 13.6.

Dividend behavior thus tells us why shares have not been a good hedge against inflation over the past decade. As inflation has accelerated, dividends declared by corporate managements have not kept pace. Any reduction in the expected growth rate of dividends in real terms will cause share values to decline, dividend yields to rise, and total returns to fall. At any moment in time different companies sell at different share price-dividend multiples, depending on their risk and on the expected future growth rate of their real dividend stream. The price-dividend multiple for the market may be viewed as a weighted average of the price-dividend ratios of individual companies. To the extent that an increase in the inflation rate lowers the expected growth rate of real dividends, the stocks of individual companies sell at lower price-dividend ratios. The market price-dividend multiple falls as a result, since the proportion of high-growth companies declines and the proportion of low-growth companies increases.[10]

In order to understand the process of equity valuation it is critically important to distinguish expected and actual share returns. Table 7-2 presents five-year averages for the components of the total return on shares over the postwar period. This clearly shows that the main reason for the low return on equities experienced since 1965 has been the negative contribution of the third component, the average rate of decline of the price-dividend ratio associated with the rise in dividend yields. This alone reduced the annual total actual return on shares by nearly 5 percent over the decade of the

---

[10] The proportional decline in price-dividend multiples will be particularly large for the rapid-growth companies. Whereas for a low-growth company a 1 percent rise in the dividend yield, say, from 9 percent to 10 percent, causes a 10 percent fall in the price-dividend ratio, from 11.1 to 10.0, for a high-growth company a 1 percent rise in the dividend yield, from 2 percent to 3 percent, causes a 33 percent fall in the price-dividend ratio, from 50.0 to 33.3.

Table 7-2: Inflation and the components of the return on shares—five-year averages (percent)

Year	$\dot{P}$	R	D/S	$\dot{S}$	$\dot{D}$	(S/D)	r	(S/P)	(D/P)	(S/D)
1975-79 . . .8.1	9.5	4.7	4.8	8.8	−4.0	1.4	− 3.3	0.6	−3.9
1970-74 . . .6.1	1.5	3.5	− 2.0	3.3	−5.3	− 4.6	− 7.9	−2.7	−5.2
1965-69 . . .3.4	6.1	3.2	3.9	5.3	−1.4	2.7	0.5	2.0	−1.5
1960-64 . . .1.2	10.9	3.2	7.7	5.6	2.1	9.7	6.4	4.3	2.1
1955-59 . . .1.6	18.9	3.9	15.0	5.4	9.6	17.3	13.1	3.5	9.6
1950-54 . . .2.5	20.4	5.8	14.6	8.2	6.4	17.9	11.8	5.6	6.2
1945-49 . . .6.4	9.8	5.1	4.7	11.0	−6.3	3.4	− 1.1	4.5	−6.6

$\dot{P}$ = Inflation rate
R = Total return (nominal) (R = D/S + S)
D/S = Dividend yield
$\dot{S}$ = Capital gains or losses (%)
$\dot{D}$ = Growth rate of dividends (%)
(S/D) = Change in price-dividend ratio
r = Real return (r ≈ R − P)
(S/P) = Growth rate of real share values
(D/P) = Growth rate of real dividends

1970s. Had the price-dividend ratio remained constant, the sum of the dividend yield and the growth rate of dividends, the expected return, was sufficient in every period to produce a positive real return on shares. Similarly, the very high total return on shares over the decade of the 1950s was due substantially to the positive contribution of the third component, which raised the annual total return on shares by about 8 percent.

Table 7-2 reveals that over the initial postwar decade, from 1945 to 1955, the expected real return on shares was about 10 percent, comprising a 5 percent dividend yield and a 5 percent growth rate of real dividends. Over the next decade, as expectations adjusted and the growth rate of real dividends was maintained above 4 percent, the dividend yield gradually fell to 3 percent, so as to generate an expected real return of about 7 percent. In the period since 1965 real dividend growth fell to below 1 percent and the dividend yield rose gradually toward 5 percent, so as to maintain expected

133

real return of 6 percent. Currently the average dividend yield is 5.5 percent and the growth rate of real dividends is positive.

This suggests that in real terms the long-run reservation supply price for equity capital lies in a range between 6 percent and 7 percent. In addition, the level will be dependent on the composition of the return between dividends and capital gains. When expected real dividend growth is very rapid and share yields are consequently low, this implies that the current price-dividend ratios will be high relative to their historic norm. As a result, while the short-run expectation of the third term, $(S/D)^e$, will always be zero, its expectation will presumably be negative for longer holding periods, to the extent that price-dividend multiples are expected to regress toward their historic norms. At such times the experienced total real return will be higher. Shareholders' reluctance to bid price-earnings multiples up further provides a floor to the dividend yield, no matter how rapid the expected growth of real dividends. Conversely, when real dividend growth is negative, share yields will be very high and current price-dividend multiples will be extremely depressed relative to their historic levels. The longer run expectation for the third component, S/D, will then be positive, to the extent that price-dividend multiples are expected to regress toward their historic levels. At such times the experienced total real return will be lower, since the depressed level of share price-dividend multiples puts a ceiling on the dividend yield, no matter how low the expected growth rate of real dividends.

Table 7-2 reveals a substantial lag between real dividend behavior and movements in the dividend yield, suggesting that expectations of real dividend growth are formed by a slow adaptive process. It took almost a decade during the immediate postwar period for the dividend yield to fall below 5 percent, despite the fact that real dividends were growing consistently at a very substantial positive rate, slowing only in the recession of 1953. Similarly, market dividend yields remained below 4 percent until the stock market collapse of

134

1974, despite the fact that real dividend growth had been negative since 1967.

Thus the outlook for the equities markets over the next decade may be seen to depend critically on the behavior of inflation. If inflation were to stabilize at its current rate of about 10 percent, real dividend growth should remain modestly positive and the current dividend yield of 5.5 percent will assure an expected real return of about 6 percent. If the rate of inflation accelerates, the real dividend growth rate will again become negative and dividend yields will rise further to generate the required expected real return, perhaps toward their historic peak of 7 percent. This implies that the price-dividend ratio will fall and that the actual total real return on shares will again be low or even negative. Nevertheless, the extent of downside risk is much more limited at present than was the case in the 1960s. The price-dividend multiple is currently about 18. Even if yields rose to their historically highest value of 7.5 percent, the price-dividend multiple would only fall to 13-14, or about 25 percent. This may be contrasted with the experience of the 1970s, when the price-dividend multiple fell from 35 to 18, or 50 percent.

Conversely, should the rate of inflation in the 1980s decline, the growth rate of real dividends might be expected to rise toward 3 or even 4 percent, depending on the extent of the deceleration, since nominal dividend growth is currently about 11 percent per year. In this scenario the dividend yield would be expected to fall slowly toward 4 percent, so as to ensure the required expected real return on shares. The price-dividend ratio would rise toward 25, an increase of about 40 percent. The actual real return would then be correspondingly higher, since the third component of the return would become positive.

It is thus possible to assess the probabilities that shares will be a good inflation hedge over the 1980s, contingent on alternative inflation rates.

1. If the inflation rate remains stable at its present level of

about 10 percent, real dividends should grow at 1-2 percent and the real return will be about 6-7 percent. The current inflation rate appears to be fully discounted in share values, so that the price-dividend ratio will remain broadly constant and share values will be maintained in real terms. By 1990 the Dow will have reached 3,000.

2. If the inflation rate accelerates to higher double-digit levels, say, 15 percent, real dividend growth will again become negative, perhaps minus 2-3 percent. The expected real return will fall toward 5 percent, and dividend yields will rise toward their historic peak value of 7 percent. Share values in real terms will decline, but by 1990 the Dow will still have exceeded 2,000.

3. If the inflation rate decelerates over the 1980s, say, to 7 percent, real dividend growth will rise to about 4-5 percent. Dividend yields will fall gradually toward 4 percent, and the expected real return on shares will rise to 8-9 percent. The price-dividend ratio will rise toward 25, and share values will more than keep up with inflation. The actual real return on shares will exceed 10 percent, and by 1990 the Dow will have exceeded 3,000.

In order to forecast share values one must be forward-looking. Actual returns will be a very poor guide to expected returns whenever the inflation rate or any other fundamental growth factors are changing rapidly. The above analysis ignored the observation that at times short-run expectations of the third component of the total return appear to be formed extrapolatively, as the market is swept by alternating moods of optimism or pessimism. As a result, no one can predict the short-run path of stock prices. But the evidence is consistent with the conclusion that the long-run expected required real return on shares lies between 5 percent and 8 percent. This, in combination with the above model, is sufficient to generate long-run forecasts of the level of equity prices.

8

The Inflation Risk and Prospective Returns for the 1980s

by

J. Anthony Boeckh
and
Richard Coghlan

THE INFLATION RISK AND PROSPECTIVE RETURNS FOR THE 1980s

*by J. Anthony Boeckh
and Richard Coghlan*

In the first chapter we briefly summarized the various views that have been put forward to explain why the stock market has done so badly in periods of inflation. In fact, it has only been in periods of accelerating inflation and tight monetary policy that the market has really been poor. We concluded that the depressing effect of accelerating inflation on the stock market resulted from the perceived risk by investors that the monetary authorities would tighten policy in order to control inflation, and that this would work by depressing the economy and the real earnings of the corporate sector. This mechanism requires an understanding of the inflationary process and the way in which monetary policy works. These are the subjects of the first four sections of this chapter, which are followed by a more detailed discussion of the relationship between market value and stock prices in the past and the lessons to be learned from that experience for the future.

Obtaining good value and making an early identification of changes in the underlying trends in the economy are the two keys to investment success. Inflation attacks both stock market value and the underlying financial trends which determine the relative attractiveness of the overall environment for equities. In light of the contributions to this book it is necessary to consider whether stocks have gone through a once-and-for-all adjustment to the new inflationary environment and are now poised to provide much higher rates of return in the future, or whether the dismal performance of the past is likely to be repeated.

Excess demand, inflation, and the balance of payments

Expressed as simply as possible, inflation is caused by excess demand. Excess demand in this context refers not only to the final demand for goods and services but also to the demand by workers for wage increases in excess of productivity gains, the demand from developers for scarce land, and so on. If demands are rising in excess of the growth of savings (at the existing level of income), then additional financing will have to be created. With limited changes in the velocity of the circulation of money (broadly defined), such demands will have to be financed by an increase in total bank credit.[1] The availability of financing can be a major constraint on expansion, real or nominal, since the new goods and services, or higher prices, have to be paid for.

The need for additional bank credit to finance an expansion of demand, whether from the private or public (i.e., government) sector, provides a means of identifying excess demand at a very early stage, and certainly before inflation takes off or the balance of payments deteriorates sharply. No single measure is going to be absolutely perfect, but certain characteristics can be defined. As far as money is concerned, the measure will have to be a broad definition which captures the role of the banks as residual providers of financing to both the public and private sectors, and their corresponding operations in the wholesale and retail money markets. It will always be difficult to know exactly where to draw the line between various liquid assets, but this may not matter too much as long as the definition is broad enough to pick up the major expansionary influences and monetary policy is operated within a free market environment, so that all interest rates move together. However, it is also necessary to look at bank credit creation, as measured, for example, by domestic

---

[1] This approach has been discussed at length in Richard Coghlan, *Money, Credit, and the Economy* (London: Allen & Unwin, 1981).

credit expansion (DCE), i.e., at bank lending directly.[2] This is likely to provide the most consistent indicator of excess demand pressure and of the likely future path of inflation, as is illustrated in Figure 8-1.

The example given in Figure 8-1 is for DCE growth and inflation in the United States, but inflation is really a global problem which affects every country. The sheer size of the

Figure 8-1

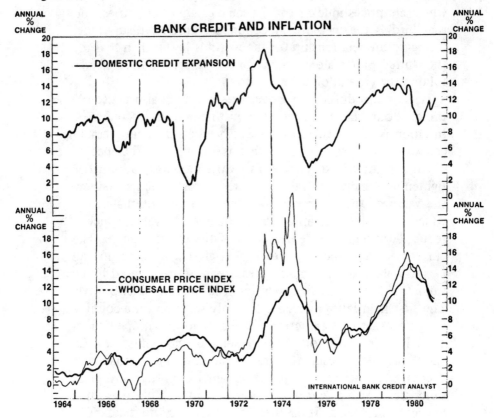

---

[2] Domestic credit expansion can be defined as additional bank lending to all domestic residents, in both the private and public sectors.

141

United States gives special importance to events in that country, but excess demand pressures originating elsewhere in the world also need to be taken into account. In order to do just that, we have constructed a *world* money supply series, based on the growth of bank credit in the main industrialized countries and weighted by the size of each economy in dollar-adjusted terms. The growth of the world money supply is shown in Figure 8-2, together with three measures of inflation: the first two are based on the weighted consumer and wholesale prices indexes for the same group of countries, and the third is the measure of commodity prices. If anything, the aggregate relationship for the world is better than that for the United States alone, although even there inflation clearly follows the growth of DCE.

Having introduced other countries, we must also say something about the relationships existing *between* countries. Inflation is one of two ways in which excess demand pressure can work its way out; the other is through the balance of payments. And both can result in the monetary authorities tightening policy. Central banks are interested in maintaining the value of their currency, whether it is the internal value, which is attacked by inflation, or the external value, which is reduced through the depreciation of the exchange rate. The current account moving into deficit gives a warning that all is not well. Excess demand pressure, whether caused by or validated through credit expansion, can show up in two ways. The first is inflation, which is the only solution for a country with no external transactions. The second, in an open economy, is a deterioration in the balance of payments. In both cases domestic residents are demanding more than the domestic economy can produce, and in both cases these outcomes are a *symptom* of fundamental imbalance—they are not the cause. It is therefore necessary to take both factors into account in assessing the likelihood that the monetary authorities will take corrective action and tighten policy.

142

Figure 8-2

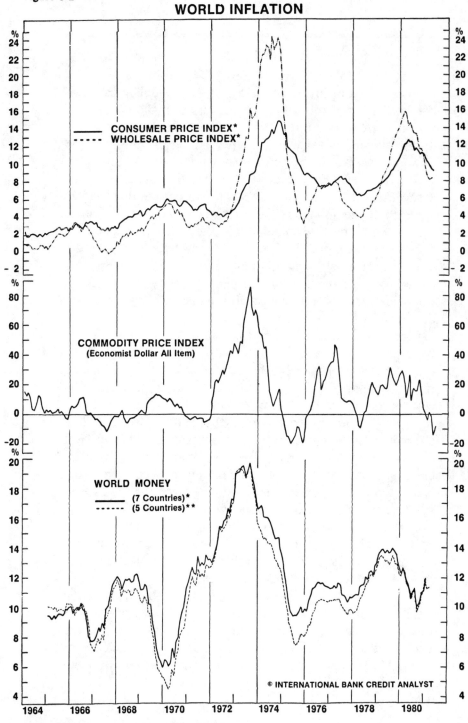

WORLD INFLATION

CONSUMER PRICE INDEX*
WHOLESALE PRICE INDEX*

COMMODITY PRICE INDEX
(Economist Dollar All Item)

WORLD MONEY
(7 Countries)*
(5 Countries)**

© INTERNATIONAL BANK CREDIT ANALYST

* The weighted sum of U.S.A., Canada, U.K., Germany, Japan,
  France and Italy.
** The weighted sum of U.S.A., Canada, U.K. Germany and Japan.

The role of monetary policy

Monetary policy is one means of controlling the excess demand pressure in the economy. Monetary policy can consist of direct controls on credit expansion in the private sector or of changes in interest rates, whose major impact is also on the private sector. Within a free market environment the only alternative open to the monetary authorities is to change interest rates. Interest rates are the market price of money, and it is through their ability to change that market price that the monetary authorities are able to influence money and credit demand. This they do by applying a squeeze on the liquidity of the banking system. Consequently, both the level of bank liquidity and the relative price of money (as summarized by the yield curve) will provide invaluable guides to the stance of monetary policy. These are discussed further below.

First, it is crucial to emphasize that monetary policy works by depressing the private industrial sector. Monetary policy can impose an intolerable burden on industry by reducing final demands for its products and sharply increasing its costs. It affects the economy and inflation by first creating a recession in the private sector. In that process profits will be slashed and, perhaps even more important, the very survival of many companies, both large and small, will become increasingly uncertain. Investors are therefore faced with falling earnings on their investments and a substantial increase in risk. At this point stock prices will be marked down. However, if such anti-inflationary policies were expected, it would only be rational for investors to discount the possibility in the present market price. This they have done, learning well from the lesson of their 1974 experience.

A major problem with monetary policy is that it leaves the public sector relatively unscathed. The public sector's greater power and authority, combined with its ability to impose taxes and its lack of any adequate measure of efficiency or profitability, enable it to crowd the private sector out of con-

144

ventional financial markets. Moreover, to compound the difficulties of the private sector, the public sector can, and has, made use of its monopoly powers to grant special tax advantages on the debt it issues and even to directly restrict credit availability to the private sector. A financial squeeze therefore impinges far more heavily on the private sector than on the public sector. And this must, of necessity, be reflected in a weak market for stocks, particularly industrial stocks.

An essential condition for economic stability and a sustained reduction in inflation is a decline in the real and financial claims of government. This would take pressure off monetary policy and allow a sustained fall in interest rates. There is evidence of a shift in this direction with the Reagan administration's emphasis on supply-side economics. It is possible to believe that the economy is at an important crossroads, but it will be some time before we find out which path has been followed. In the meantime, emphasis will remain on monetary policy, as the government's borrowing requirements will remain huge for a lengthy period.

If tightening credit conditions are going to have an adverse effect on stock prices, investors should try to anticipate them as early as possible. There are three basic indicators they can use. The first requirement is some indicator of future policy action. The importance given to inflation by the monetary authorities means that this must provide the main leading indicator. We would argue that recognition of this fact accounts for rising earnings yields (falling P/Es) in times of inflation. It also explains why the older capital-intensive sectors will do relatively badly, particularly if product sales rely heavily on credit and are affected by foreign competition (e.g., the automobile industry).

However, as we noted above, inflation is not the only way in which excess demand shows up. The alternative is for the external balance of payments to deteriorate. In West Germany, for example, the earnings yield reached 14 percent in 1980, paralleling the level achieved in the United States, but with inflation as measured by consumer prices never exceeding 6 percent. The rise in the earnings yield was associated with rising short-term interest rates and, in particular, with an inversion of the yield curve. West Germany's main concern was the worsening balance of payments on current account, which deteriorated through 1979 and 1980, reaching an annual total of around DM30 billion ($14 billion). That rise in the current account deficit was just as clear a signal of impending corrective monetary policy as soaring inflation would have been.

A second requirement is to have some indicator of future inflation. Monetary policy, as we have seen, is directed at the credit demands of the private sector, but those demands are not the only cause of inflation. The government's fiscal policy and its policy toward intervention in foreign exchange markets are also important determinants of inflation, as are certain external shocks over which the government has no control. In short, what is required as a guide to future inflation is some broad measure of money or DCE, which was discussed above.

The third requirement, which is crucial in identifying cyclical turning points, is to determine the stance of monetary policy. The two indicators we emphasized in our discussion of monetary policy were relative interest rates (i.e., the yield curve), and private sector liquidity. We will now consider these indicators in more detail.

The yield curve

It is clear that the level of nominal interest rates cannot be used to measure the tightness or ease of monetary policy during a period of inflation. It is also impossible to measure a "true" rate of interest after allowing for the *expected* rate of inflation over the investors' desired holding period. A good measure of the stance of monetary policy is the yield curve. In simple terms, this can be measured by the relationship between short-term and long-term interest rates. The yield curve is said to be inverted when short rates are above long

146

rates, a consistently accurate indication of tight money. During recessions and the early stages of economic recoveries the yield curve is positive (i.e., short rates are below long rates), implying easy, or at least cheap, money. During the late stages of the recovery cycle, when inflation is strong and monetary policy has been forced to tighten sharply, short rates rise and the yield curve usually becomes inverted. The degree of inversion is a good proxy for the degree of monetary tightness in the absence of credit controls. As can be seen in Figure 8-3, inverted yield curves have tended to precede downturns in economic activity, being closely associated with periods of declining stock prices. In recent years the degree of inversion has been increased by the gradual dismantling of credit controls, interest rate ceilings, and restraints on competition in financial markets. Lately this process has been speeded up, and the effect has been to put more pressure on the price of credit (i.e., interest rates) to clear the financial markets. The effects on demand are the same, but the process and the visible signs of stress are different. With more emphasis on the price of credit, interest rates will have to be pushed higher and stay there longer.

The yield curve, in an important sense, reflects expectations about what will happen to short-term interest rates in the future. If inflation increases, this will influence expectations about the inflationary outlook and result in an increase in long-term interest rates, as lenders seek compensation for the loss of principal resulting from the higher actual and/or expected inflation rate. If short rates do not also rise, then borrowers will turn to the short end of the market, where costs are lower. This, in turn, will push up short rates. If the monetary authorities then tighten liquidity in order to bring inflation under control, short-term interest rates will be pushed up even further. The extent to which short rates are pushed up relative to long rates will depend on the resolve of the monetary authorities as reflected in the tightness of monetary policy, while the level that interest rates have to reach will be determined by the rate of inflation itself.

147

Figure 8-3

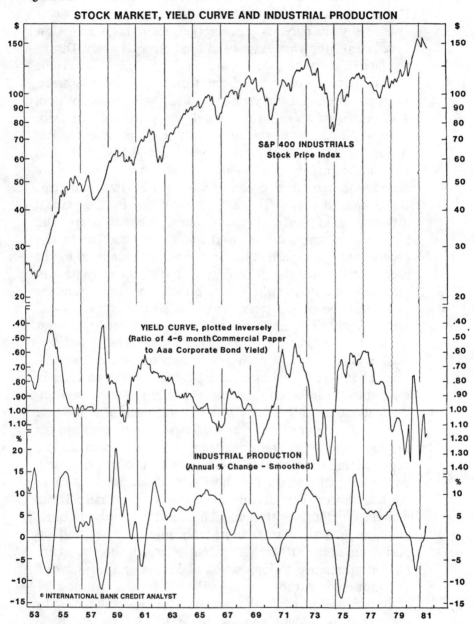

STOCK MARKET, YIELD CURVE AND INDUSTRIAL PRODUCTION

S&P 400 INDUSTRIALS
Stock Price Index

YIELD CURVE, plotted inversely
(Ratio of 4–6 month Commercial Paper
to Aaa Corporate Bond Yield)

INDUSTRIAL PRODUCTION
(Annual % Change – Smoothed)

© INTERNATIONAL BANK CREDIT ANALYST

148

Nominal interest rates viewed in isolation are potentially misleading.

As liquidity is tightened and short rates are pushed up, the initial effect will also be to depress bond prices and the equity market. Bond prices, however, will be dominated by expectations about inflation, and firm and credible action by the monetary authorities in the present will eventually serve to improve expectations about inflation in the future. Tightening credit conditions will therefore be reflected in an increase in short rates *relative to* long rates and in an increasingly inverted, or negative, yield curve. Monetary policy will then have to remain tight, and the yield curve inverted, until there is a cyclical downturn in short-term credit demands.

When short-term interest rates rise significantly above long-term rates *and remain there,* they make short-term credit expensive and raise doubts about whether the increased cost can be passed on. As long as short-term interest rates are expected to fall quickly, the contractionary effect will be slight. Short-term interest rates have to remain high, and the yield curve inverted, long enough to create the expectation that they will stay that way for a long time. Paradoxically, it is only then that short-term interest rates can start to come down substantially. Essentially, monetary policy will reduce inflation by creating a recession. There is no alternative—that is the only way to reduce private sector credit demands, given fiscal policy. Therefore, interest rates can only come down when they have achieved that objective. If the earnings yield did not rise with inflation, and remained roughly constant in this correction phase, then as earnings come under severe downward pressure stock prices would also have to fall sharply in order to maintain the earnings yield. It is therefore entirely rational for investors to anticipate the correction, to a large extent if not entirely, by reducing the price they are prepared to pay for any current level of earnings, thereby pushing up the earnings yield with inflation.

Rates of change of liquidity

The other measure of monetary policy we would like to emphasize here is changing balance sheet liquidity in the private sector. When bank and corporate liquidity are improving—normally after a recession, when bank loans are declining, inflation is decelerating, and monetary policy has eased—stock prices are generally very strong. Late in the business cycle, when inflation is accelerating, bank loans rise sharply and monetary policy tightens. What is relevant for securities markets is the rate of change of liquidity. Securities markets seem to be able to adjust to a given level of liquidity, but they react when liquidity begins to change for better or worse.

There are many ways to measure liquidity changes in the banking system. Our purpose here is not to catalog these various indicators but simply to point out that they are important tools for assessing the macroeconomic environment for stock prices. What we have found over the years is that the various indicators of liquidity changes do not perform consistently from cycle to cycle. Hence, lead times can vary. It is best to combine the various indicators into a consensus indicator which reduces lead times as much as possible but at the same time minimizes the risk of mistakes. Such a consensus indicator, called the Monetary Thermometer, has been used for many years in the *Bank Credit Analyst*.[3] Constructed from 10 individual indicators, it was based on data going back to 1919 in order to cover as many cycles as possible. The indicators of the Monetary Thermometer are summarized in Table 8-4. From historical experience certain criteria were established for each indicator as it moved through various degrees of deterioration. One, two, or three demerit points are assigned when respective degrees of deterioration are hit. For example, if an indicator drops 10 percent, one demerit point might be assigned; if it falls 25 percent, it

---

[3] This indicator was also discussed in H. Bolton, *Money and Investment Profits* (Homewood, Ill.: Dow Jones-Irwin, 1967). The *Bank Credit Analyst* is a monthly stock market and investment publication.

Table 8-1

MONETARY THERMOMETER

INDICATOR		1976	1977	1978	1979	1980	
		J F M A M J J A S O N D	J F M A M J J A S O N D	J F M A M J J A S O N D	J F M A M J J A S O N D	J F M A M J J A S O N D	J F M A M J
P O L I C Y	N.Y.S.E. Stock Margins						
	N.Y. Discount Rate		████████	████████████	████████████	██ ███████	
	Bank Reserve Requirements						
B A N K I N G	Financial Flow		██████████	████████████	████████████	████	
	Cyclical Banking Liquidity		████████	████████████	████████████		
	Bank Investments						
T R A N S A C T I O N	Debit/ Loan Ratio		███████	████████████	███████████	██	
	Revised Composite Equity		██████	████████████	████████████	██	
C O M B I N E D	Original Bank Credit Barometer						
	Revised Bank Credit Barometer		████	████████████	████████████	████████████	████
TEMPERATURE		0 0 0 0 0 0 0 0 0 0 0 0	0 0 0 0 0 0 0 0 1 4 5 8	8 9 10 11 11 11 13 16 16 17 17 17	17 18 18 18 18 18 18 18 18 18 18 18	18 18 18 18 12 6 6 5 5 4 5 6	6 6 6 6 6 6

might be assigned two demerit points; and if it is off 50 percent, it might receive the full complement of three demerit points. This is a rather arbitrary technique, but it is effective when a number of indicators are used together to get a consensus measure like the Monetary Thermometer.

The maximum reading is therefore 30, and the minimum, that is, the most bullish, is 0. Empirically, 8 has been considered the warning level. Thus readings of 8 or higher are considered to indicate a credit environment that is cyclically unfavorable for stock prices, and conversely for readings from 0 to 7.

Figure 8-4 shows the long-term record of the Monetary Thermometer back to 1919. The shaded areas represent readings that are in the "bearish" 8 or higher category.

The outlook for the 1980s

One can look at a number of things to get a handle on whether stocks are cheap, expensive, or fairly valued. Looked at in isolation, stocks appear to be fairly valued at present— neither obviously cheap nor expensive.

On an income basis, stocks appear to be priced to provide an underlying nominal rate of return (abstracting from short-term price fluctuations) of between 15 percent and 20 percent. While this is well above the historic figure of 9-10 percent, it is not high in terms of today's inflation and taxation rates and the obviously high level of uncertainty and risk.

There are several ways in which one can estimate the potential return on stocks using, for example, the S&P 400 as a benchmark. For example, the underlying rate of return on equities is approximately equal to the dividend yield plus the growth in dividends, assuming no change in expectations of risk and attitudes toward risk. If one assumes that the underlying real growth rate of the U.S. economy is about 3 percent and the underlying inflation rate is about 10 percent, then corporate earnings and dividends should grow by about 13 percent on balance, abstracting from cyclical considera-

152

Figure 8-4

THE MONETARY THERMOMETER AND THE MARKET

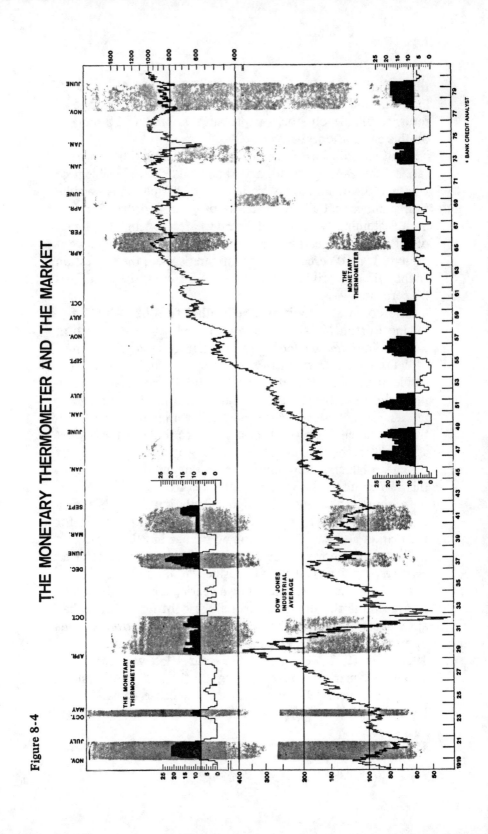

THE MONETARY THERMOMETER

DOW JONES INDUSTRIAL AVERAGE

THE MONETARY THERMOMETER

* BANK CREDIT ANALYST

tions. Since the dividend yield on the S&P at the time of writing is around 4 percent, then the expected underlying rate of return available on stocks is probably around 18-20 percent on this calculation.

Another calculation can be made by adding the inflation rate to the earnings yield, and thus avoiding the problem of whether dividend payout ratios are distorted. This calculation assumes that all dividends are paid out and that firms are on a sustaining basis only if earnings are growing at the rate of inflation. The earnings-price ratio is around 11 percent at present. If a 10 percent inflation figure is used, the suggestion is that the underlying return on stocks could be as high as 21 percent.

One could also look at a bellwether firm like AT&T, following Burton Malkiel (Chapter 5), and say that its return was a minimum expected for the market as a whole, since AT&T is at the low end of the risk spectrum. For AT&T the dividend yield is around 10 percent, and a conservative estimate of the expected growth rate using the lower range of brokerage estimates is 6 percent, suggesting an expected return to shareholders of at least 16 percent. Thus the market as a whole should provide something in excess of that. If AT&T's dividend grew at the same rate in the 1980s as in the 1970s, then the return would be around 17½ percent.

In short, this type of rough calculation suggests that a return of at least 18 percent is a reasonable expectation for the market as a whole, assuming no change in P/E ratios.

Table 8-2 shows actual experience of reported aftertax earnings, dividends, the GNE business price deflator, current cost retained earnings (excluding a gearing adjustment to take into account the depreciation of net debt in corporate balance sheets), and price-deflated stock prices over various intervals back to 1952. Demarcation years for the intervals of 1965 and 1972 were used. The year 1965 was significant because it marked the beginning of the fall in real stock prices. The year 1972 was significant because it marked the beginning of rapid inflation. Several interesting facts emerge.

154

Table 8-2: Earnings, dividends, and prices in the non-financial corporate sector (compound per annum growth rates)

	1952-80	1952-65	1965-80	1972-80
Reported aftertax earnings	7.6%	5.1%	8.1%	13.6%
Dividends	6.9	6.3	7.4	11.7
GNE business price deflator	4.4	2.7	6.0	7.4
Current cost retained earnings . . .	5.2	12.5	−0.4	−0.9
Price-deflated stock prices	1.5	7.7	−3.6	−6.6

First, reported aftertax profits in the nonfinancial corporate sector exceeded price inflation over each of the intervals by a substantial margin. In particular, from 1972 to 1980, when inflation was greatest, profits rose almost twice as fast as inflation. Dividends also rose faster than price inflation in all periods, particularly from 1952 to 1965 and from 1972 to 1980. It is also interesting to note the reasonably close relationship between current cost retained earnings and deflated stock prices. From 1952 to 1980 and from 1952 to 1965, both rose, though the rise in earnings was faster than the rise in real stock prices by about 4-5 percentage points. Taken over either the 1965-80 period or just the 1972-80 period, current cost earnings fell marginally. Real stock prices fell somewhat more. The differential between the two, however, didn't change much, being 3.2 and 5.7 percentage points in the two periods, respectively.

The conclusion that one can draw from Table 8-1 is that dividends can grow faster than inflation on a sustained basis. Ignoring the extremely low stock market readings of 1974, stock prices were able to rise about as fast as inflation over this period, suggesting that firms were able to index their earnings. Thus stocks, properly priced, appear to be an effective inflation hedge, since firms can pay dividends that will more than keep up with inflation. For example, should dividends continue to rise at the 1972-80 rate, then stock market returns would come in at close to 17 percent, assuming constant P/Es. Should inflation abate, the P/E ratio could well move up. The negative side is that, should inflation accelerate, current cost earnings and real stock prices would probably fall, as they did from 1972 to 1980, and hence the actual return to shareholders would be less than the sum of the dividend yield and the dividend growth rate.

In short, stocks appear to be capable of providing a reasonable pretax return to shareholders, assuming no major discontinuities in the economic and financial system, that is, if one rules out crashes or sharply accelerating inflation. The basic assumption required is that over the next five years inflation remain in a range of 8-12 percent most of the time, with 10 percent being the central tendency. Shareholder earnings should then grow at least as fast as inflation.

Shareholder returns also have to be compared with returns to bondholders. Comparable bonds would be reasonably high-quality issues of long-term maturity. These are currently yielding around 16 percent. Thus it would appear that equities are providing a pretax risk premium of approximately 300 basis points or more. The aftertax risk premium would be somewhat larger, as part of the return to shareholders comes as a capital gain. Such a risk premium appears to be about right in the environment that is most likely to exist in the next few years. Thus a comparison with bonds also suggests that stocks are reasonably priced at present, assuming no dramatic changes in the business environment.

Stock values can also be looked at from a balance sheet point of view. The most appropriate measure is market price relative to book value on a replacement cost basis. Any commodity can sell above or below its replacement cost for lengthy periods, but sooner or later the underlying laws of economics must prevail and market prices must bear some relationship to production costs. Sugar, for example, sold well below production costs in the 1960s. Capital stock can also sell above or below its production costs. However, it is distinguished from most commodities by its long production time and its long lifetime in use. Therefore, the supply and demand adjustment process can take much longer. Thus valuation can never be a very precise procedure. Moreover, foreign competition and government tax and regulation policy can seriously affect economic and hence market values, and thus comparisons with domestic replacement costs can be very misleading, particularly for individual companies and industries. For the total industrial sector, however, many of the distortions are averaged out, and thus the relationship between market price and replacement book value can be very useful, particularly if it is used in conjunction with the rate of return data on replacement book value.

Figure 8-5 shows the S&P 400 industrial stock prices, the historical and current cost book values of the corporate sector, and the premium or discount of stock prices from replacement cost book value. In the early postwar period an enormous discount from replacement book value appeared, running to almost 70 percent in the 1949 bear market low. The discount narrowed progressively, moving to a premium for most of the 1960s. The peak premium occurred in 1968, at 23 percent. Subsequently, a series of sharp market declines coinciding with accelerating inflation created a return to deep discounts. At the 1974 market low the discount was approximately 60 percent, exceeded only once during the postwar period. Even though stock prices moved up sharply in 1975 and 1976, the discount remained large. It then widened after 1976, as stock prices weakened and inflation accelerated again. By the end of 1980 the discount approximated 40 percent.

An obvious question is, Why, compared with the 1960s, are stock prices so low relative to their replacement book value? This can be seen in the upper panel of Figure 8-6, which shows the rate of return on replacement book value. At its peak, in 1966, this profit ratio was about 8½ percent, which explains the large premium over replacement book value then. As of the end of 1980, the ratio is around 3½ percent. Except for the second half of 1974, this is the lowest reading in the postwar period and explains much of why the discount on replacement book value was around

Figure 8-5

NOMINAL AND REAL STOCK MARKET INDEX AND A MEASURE OF BOOK VALUE

Standard & Poor's 400 Industrials
(Monthly Average)

Real Standard & Poor's 400 Industrials*

Premium/Discount of Equity Market Value
against Current Cost Book Value

Premium
Discount

Premium
Discount

© BANK CREDIT ANALYST

Source: U.S. Dept. of Commerce
Federal Reserve System
Standard & Poor's Corp.

*STANDARD & POOR'S 400 INDUSTRIALS (MONTHLY AVERAGE) DEFLATED BY GNP PRICE DEFLATOR.

158

40 percent. In effect, the true profitability ratio demonstrates that *on average* the economic value of the underlying assets of corporations is less than replacement value. In extreme cases, where, for example, a plant is closed, the economic value is effectively zero, whereas the replacement value recorded by the Department of Commerce would be a significant positive figure until the write-off.

The point to note is that returns on assets which are inflating in price generally fall below long-term norms during inflations. This is acceptable to most investors if the asset they own appreciates. Real estate is the prime example.

The same is now true of equities. Investors are prepared to hold them at current levels even though the current cost profit on the replacement book value of their equities is around 3-4 percent. Part of the reason is that the discount from replacement book value is such that stocks can be expected to at least keep pace with inflation at current levels. As discussed earlier, the expected returns to shareholders at present appear to be about 18-20 percent over a reasonable holding period. In short, stock prices have fallen far enough to reflect the relatively low rate of return on a current cost basis.

From whichever way we approach this question, the basic conclusion is that stocks as a group are about properly valued if future returns are consistent with the returns currently implied by prices and if expected risk remains about the same. In other words, the real rate of return on invested capital (at replacement cost) available to the equity shareholders is around 6 percent at present, when account is taken of the approximately 40 percent discount at which stocks are selling. This relationship can be seen in the lower panel of Figure 8-6, which adjusts the rate of return for the discount on replacement book value. The return would be around 8 percent if it were adjusted cyclically for the relatively depressed state of the economy in 1980-81. This return is not far out of line with the postwar average, and it appears reasonable from an

Figure 8-6

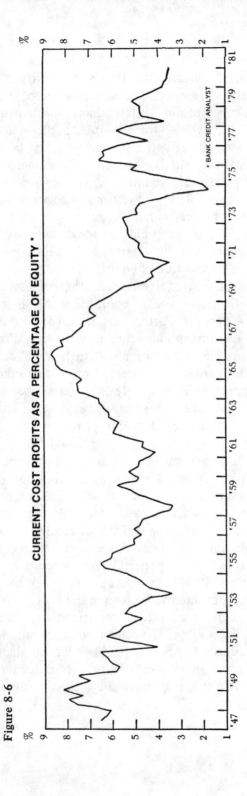

CURRENT COST PROFITS AS A PERCENTAGE OF EQUITY *

* BANK CREDIT ANALYST

Figure 8-6 *(continued)*

CURRENT COST PROFITS AS A PERCENTAGE OF EQUITY *
ADJUSTED FOR PREMIUM/DISCOUNT ON REPLACEMENT BOOK VALUE

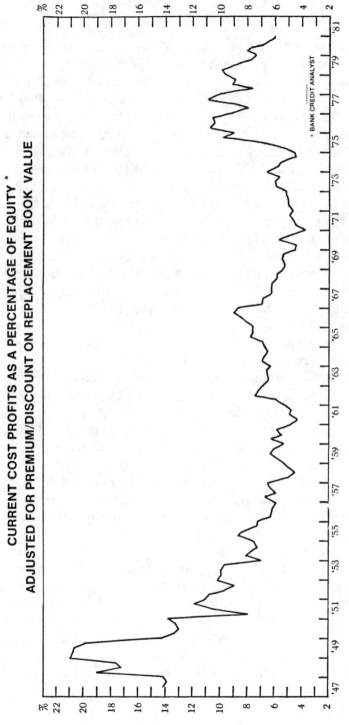

© BANK CREDIT ANALYST

* After Tax Profits adjusted for IVA, CCA & Gearing divided by Current Cost Net Worth

intuitive point of view since it allows for some risk premium over the real returns available on corporate bonds.

Real returns fell sharply from their inflated levels of the mid-1960s to the exaggeratedly low point of late 1974, as can be seen in Figure 8-6. As a result, stock prices fell dramatically. Thus actual shareholder experience confirmed suspicions that stocks were a disaster in a period of accelerating inflation. However, the experience of the last five years provides a totally different perspective. Adjusted for cyclicality, and removing the extreme experience of late 1974, the current cost rate of return is not much less than it was during the period 1950-63. As time goes by and confidence develops that stocks can continue to provide a reasonable real rate of return during a prolonged period of inflation, investors may be willing to pay more for equities than would be justified by risk considerations. This has in fact happened with real estate, precious metals, and other inflation hedges that have a track record of providing acceptable real rates of return during an inflationary period.

In sum, one can say that if future experience in the financial world falls within the confines of the experience of the last 10 years, then the average level of stock prices is neither a bargain nor excessively expensive. Over time, if cyclically adjusted real returns of corporations remain around the level of the last five years or improve either for basic economic reasons or for other reasons, such as the reduction in the corporate and personal tax burdens introduced by the new administration, then stock prices should improve relative to their underlying current cost asset values.

Moreover, as long as a large discount from replacement book exists, tremendous arbitrage possibilities through mergers and acquisitions will remain, and this will prevent stock prices from getting too far out of line with underlying asset value. Also, to the extent that firms buy underlying assets from other firms rather than invest in new plant and equipment because the return is too low, the potential for rising returns on invested capital is enhanced. In other words, the

162

bigger the discount from replacement cost and the longer it goes on, the more certain investors can be that returns must rise. The overinvestment of the 1960s, reflecting very high returns, gave way to the excessively low returns and underinvestment of the 1970s. The reverse is almost certain to occur in the 1980s, barring major shocks and more than normal policy errors by government officials and politicians.

It should also be noted that even though stocks sell at a big discount from replacement book value, mergers and acquisition arbitrage cannot function continuously. During credit crunches and debt deflation crises, inability to get financing can cause a suspension of such activity, leaving even cheap stocks vulnerable for a time.

Conclusions

The overall level of the stock market will be affected by cyclical movements of the economy. Prices will rise at times of easy money and low interest rates, which provide a stimulus to economic growth. As interest rates rise and money tightens, so the business environment will worsen; costs will rise, demand will fall, profits will be squeezed from both sides, and stock prices will become depressed.

Inevitably, the more that the tightening comes as a surprise to the market, the more prices will fall. Consequently, the stock market was much more vulnerable in 1972 and 1973 when the earnings yield was only 5 percent than it was at the end of the 1970s when the earnings yield was above 10 percent. The sharp credit tightening in 1973 and 1974 took the market by surprise and prices had to fall substantially in order to discount the inflated earnings. Following that experience, investors allowed inflated earnings to increase the earnings yield. This provided a cushion, although not complete protection, against the depressing effects of the inevitable period of tight money which followed. The need for a correction had already been discounted to a large extent as investors reacted rationally to what seemed to be a nonsus-

163

tainable situation. However, the market can never fully escape from credit tightening. It just becomes less sensitive when it has already discounted the need for some tightening because investors have correctly read the trend in the economy, inflation, credit demands, and money supply growth.

The key to investment success in the future, as in the past, will depend on investors' ability to (a) assess value and prospective rates of return in an environment of fluctuating inflation rates, and (b) the macro-economic environment which will determine whether credit conditions will be expansionary or contractionary and whether inflation will be accelerating or decelerating.

Our view in 1981 is that the world will remain in an environment of relative disinflation for an extended period primarily because interest rates will remain high, relative to both past norms and inflation, since the Federal Reserve and other central banks will be much less willing to finance excessive credit demands. Thus, the traditional inflation hedges will probably not be nearly as rewarding as they were in the 1970s, and might even be very disappointing. Fixed-income securities will be relatively more rewarding than they have been, especially compared with inflation. They will, however, continue to be volatile and risky until it is certain that inflation is headed permanently lower.

The stock market, on the other hand, appears to be fairly valued at present and should provide returns of around 18-20 percent over a reasonable holding period if the United States can avoid a catastrophic deflationary or inflationary crisis. If inflation averages between 8 percent and 12 percent over the next 5 years, then equities should provide a return that will be substantially higher than the rate of inflation.

As long as the emphasis remains on monetary policy to fight inflation, with no support from fiscal policy, the upside potential of the stock market will be limited. Only if the corporate sector is stimulated by new supply-side policies—tax reduction, deregulation, and enlightened energy policies—and inflation and interest rates begin a secular decline through

164

permanently reduced budget deficits and tighter, more consistent monetary policies, will earnings yields fall back toward historic norms. Under these circumstances the 40-50 percent discount on replacement book value set by the stock market over the past 7 years will be reduced and could even turn over to a premium, as in the 1960s.

Investors must recognize that there will be continuing cyclicality in the economy, inflation, and the market. From the sorts of broad financial indicators discussed earlier, such as DCE and world money supply, the yield curve, and the Monetary Thermometer, it will be evident whether monetary policy is too tight or too easy, and whether balance sheets have become more liquid or less liquid. Anticipating the broad fluctuations in markets will require a continuous monitoring of such indicators of financial flows and monetary policy. These indicators will also be critical in gauging whether the secular trend of inflation and interest rates will be downward and, hence, whether the overall financial system will undergo the sort of structural improvement that is necessary for a sustained increase in real stock prices.